D0948940

The Homicide Detective

Other titles in the Crime Scene Investigations series:

The Homicide Detective

by Toney Allman

LUCENT BOOKS
A part of Gale, Cengage Learning

GALE
CENGAGE Learning

Detroit • New York • San Francisco • New Haven, Conn • Waterville, Maine • London

LIBRARY OF CONGRESS CATALOGING-IN-PUBLICATION DATA

Allman, Toney.
  The homicide detective / by Toney Allman.
    p. cm. -- (Crime scene investigations)
  Includes bibliographical references and index.
  ISBN 978-1-4205-0109-4 (hardcover)
1. Murder--Investigation--Juvenile literature. 2. Homicide investigation--Juvenile literature. 3. Detectives--Juvenile literature. 4. Criminal investigation--Juvenile literature. I. Title.
  HV8079.H6A46 2009
  363.25'952--dc22

           2009017987

Lucent Books
27500 Drake Rd
Farmington Hills MI 48331

ISBN-13: 978-1-4205-0109-4
ISBN-10: 1-4205-0109-7

Printed in the United States of America
1 2 3 4 5 6 7 13 12 11 10 09

Printed by Bang Printing, Brainerd, MN, 1st Ptg., 11/2009

Contents

Foreword

The popularity of crime scene and investigative crime shows on television has come as a surprise to many who work in the field. The main surprise is the concept that crime scene analysts are the true crime solvers, when in truth, it takes dozens of people, doing many different jobs, to solve a crime. Often, the crime scene analyst's contribution is a small one. One Minnesota forensic scientist says that the public "has gotten the wrong idea. Because I work in a lab similar to the ones on *CSI*, people seem to think I'm solving crimes left and right—just me and my microscope. They don't believe me when I tell them that it's just the investigators that are solving crimes, not me."

Crime scene analysts do have an important role to play, however. Science has rapidly added a whole new dimension to gathering and assessing evidence. Modern crime labs can match a hair of a murder suspect to one found on a murder victim, for example, or recover a latent fingerprint from a threatening letter, or use a powerful microscope to match tool marks made during the wiring of an explosive device to a tool in a suspect's possession.

Probably the most exciting of the forensic scientist's tools is DNA analysis. DNA can be found in just one drop of blood, a dribble of saliva on a toothbrush, or even the residue from a fingerprint. Some DNA analysis techniques enable scientists to tell with certainty, for example, whether a drop of blood on a suspect's shirt is that of a murder victim.

While these exciting techniques are now an essential part of many investigations, they cannot solve crimes alone. "DNA doesn't come with a name and address on it," says the Minnesota forensic scientist. "It's great if you have someone in custody to match the sample to, but otherwise, it doesn't help.

That's the investigator's job. We can have all the great DNA evidence in the world, and without a suspect, it will just sit on a shelf. We've all seen cases with very little forensic evidence get solved by the resourcefulness of a detective."

While forensic specialists get the most media attention today, the work of detectives still forms the core of most criminal investigations. Their job, in many ways, has changed little over the years. Most cases are still solved through the persistence and determination of a criminal detective whose work may be anything but glamorous. Many cases require routine, even mind-numbing tasks. After the July 2005 bombings in London, for example, police officers sat in front of video players watching thousands of hours of closed-circuit television tape from security cameras throughout the city, and as a result were able to get the first images of the bombers.

The Lucent Books Crime Scene Investigations series explores the variety of ways crimes are solved. Titles cover particular crimes such as murder, specific cases such as the killing of three civil rights workers in Mississippi, or the role specialists such as medical examiners play in solving crimes. Each title in the series demonstrates the ways a crime may be solved, from the various applications of forensic science and technology to the reasoning of investigators. Sidebars examine both the limits and possibilities of the new technologies and present crime statistics, career information, and step-by-step explanations of scientific and legal processes.

The Crime Scene Investigations series strives to be both informative and realistic about how members of law enforcement—criminal investigators, forensic scientists, and others—solve crimes, for it is essential that student researchers understand that crime solving is rarely quick or easy. Many factors—from a detective's dogged pursuit of one tenuous lead to a suspect's careless mistakes to sheer luck to complex calculations computed in the lab—are all part of crime solving today.

Murder Specialists

In almost every large city, the police force has a homicide squad, homicide unit, or homicide division made up of detectives who specialize in death investigations. These men and women usually have been members of the police force for several years. They have been officers on the street or in patrol cars and have answered calls for help and responded to all kinds of criminal activities. They have proven their abilities as cops. They are skilled in their jobs and are wise in the ways of criminals.

Should officers decide that they want to become detectives, they can request consideration from superiors, and in some cases take an examination that demonstrates their abilities. Should they want to become homicide detectives, they must be appointed by the homicide division's supervisor, lieutenant, or commander, depending on the city. Once accepted, new homicide detectives are paired with seasoned, experienced homicide detectives so that they can learn how to do their jobs. They acquire practical experience and learn investigation techniques from their experienced partners.

Homicide detectives are responsible for investigating violent deaths, identifying killers, and bringing the murderers to justice. No matter how difficult, they must try to find out the truth about homicides. No matter who the victims are, they deserve the best efforts of homicide detectives. Homicide detectives want to arrest the right people and obtain justice for the victims.

Former New York homicide detective Vernon J. Geberth is the author of a respected manual about how to conduct homicide investigations. At the beginning of the manual is an oath

Homicide detectives specialize in murder and bringing the killer or killers to justice.

that describes the right way to approach a homicide. It voices Geberth's belief that solving homicides is a solemn obligation. The oath says:

"Homicide investigation is a profound duty. As an officer entrusted with such a duty, it is incumbent upon you [required of you] to develop an understanding of the dynamics and principles of professional homicide investigation....

Death investigation constitutes a heavy responsibility, and as such, let no person deter you from the truth and your own personal commitment to see that justice is done. Not only for the deceased, but for the surviving family as well."[1]

CHAPTER 1

Called to the Scene

Detective Curt Brannan received a telephone call from police dispatch on a Monday evening in May 1997. Police officers had responded to a 911 call about a death and discovered the body of Brenda Salazar, a twenty-year-old Hispanic woman, in the Fort Worth, Texas, apartment she shared with her roommate. The roommate, Jennifer Ledesma, had just returned home after a weekend visit with her family. She discovered Salazar's body as she entered their apartment and called for help immediately. It was easy for responding officers to determine that they were at the scene of a murder. Salazar could not have placed herself in the position in which she was found. Her hands were tied behind her back, and a ligature, a constricting leather strap, was around her neck. Following standard procedure, the police officers called their headquarters and requested that a homicide detective respond to the scene as soon as possible. They protected the crime scene until Detective Brannan arrived.

Taking Charge

Homicide detectives respond to all reports of unexpected deaths, including natural deaths, suicides, deaths due to accidents, and homicides. If the cause of Brenda Salazar's death had not been evident to the responding officers, then Brannan may have gone to the scene alone. But since they suspected a homicide, Brannan phoned his supervisor, Sergeant Paul Kratz, and both men headed for the murder scene.

Brannan arrived at the apartment building first. The responding patrol officers had already secured the crime scene. The apartment was roped off so that no one could enter.

Officers had the witnesses, including the roommate, waiting for Brannan so that he could question them. Now the officers were waiting outside the apartment, ready to tell Brannan what had occurred so far.

First responding officers secure the scene with crime tape to avoid contamination.

Brannan did not rush inside to see the body. First, he looked slowly around the area of the apartment building. He noticed the nearby swimming pool, the apartment office, and the location of the apartment that was the murder scene. He noticed the crowd of onlookers who had gathered. He called over one of the police officers and asked for information. He took out his notebook and made notes as Officer William Bench described what the roommate had told him about finding the body. He took more notes as Bench described the scene he had found inside the apartment. He satisfied himself through his questioning of Bench that the crime scene had been secured immediately and appropriately. He learned that the victim's car had been found by other police officers several miles away.

In addition to his notes, he spoke into a tape recorder, describing what he had learned.

Then Brannan issued his first instructions. He asked the officers to make a list of the license-plate numbers of every car in the apartment building's parking lot. He also asked them to get the name and phone number of every onlooker at the scene.

This was Brannan's murder to solve, and he would gather any and all information that he could. He would not let any possible evidence slip away or be overlooked while the scene was still fresh. If, for example, the murderer was hanging around watching the activity, Brannan would not miss the opportunity to get his name.

An Awesome Responsibility

Experienced homicide detectives often say that the body can wait. It is not going anywhere. Other evidence, however, may disappear. The detective cannot know in advance what information may be important to the investigation, so he or she tries to absorb as much information as possible from the moment a dead body is found. From those first moments, explains former

A detective interviews responding officers and documents it in her notebook. It is necessary for detectives to take careful notes and document every step in case there is a trial.

Chalk Fairies

Detective Vernon J. Geberth calls overeager officers who draw a chalk line around murder victims "chalk fairies." He says, "'Chalk fairy' is a term used to describe mysterious police officers who feel the need to draw lines around the body and then disappear when investigators attempt to find out who contaminated the scene." Sometimes, bodies need to be removed quickly from crime scenes. At those times, chalk lines that show the position of the victim at the scene are necessary. However, a homicide detective will be very upset when a chalk line is drawn around a dead body by responding officers if it is not necessary (which is why no one will admit to having done it). The detective has to have photographs taken of the scene *before* it is changed in any way. Otherwise, the photo shows a crime scene that is altered, or contaminated. The photo is no longer an accurate representation of the victim. In court, defense lawyers have successfully prevented such photographs from being used as evidence. The judge rules them inadmissible, because they are not true pictures of the original crime scene.

Vernon J. Geberth, *Practical Homicide Investigation*, Boca Raton, FL: CRC Press, 1996, p. 49.

New York homicide detective Vernon J. Geberth, "our mission is to bring justice to the deceased and their surviving family. We do this by conducting a professional and intelligent investigation which results in the identification and apprehension of the killer and the successful prosecution of the case."[2] The mission is a large one, requiring a homicide detective to be in charge of the investigation, from beginning to end. He or she "owns" the case.

With the help of a team of crime-scene specialists, a detective must make decisions that will guide the investigation in identifying the killer or killers and ensuring a successful arrest. The responsibility includes conducting an investigation that is constitutionally legal and results in evidence that is admissible in a court of law. The homicide detective has many rules to follow. He or she must document actions at every step so that, should it be necessary, the evidence can be presented at a trial. Geberth explains that a homicide detective must be "street-smart and book-wise" and possess "experience, flexibility, and common sense."[3]

At the Salazar crime scene, Brannan interviewed the responding officers and issued his instructions with all of these requirements in mind. He made notes of his actions that could be used as documentation should he find the killer and need the evidence when the killer went to trial. Only after he had ensured that nothing would be missed outside did Brannan move on to the apartment itself and step inside. He was ready to continue gathering evidence in this careful, methodical way as he viewed the body of the homicide victim. What he did at the crime scene could very well determine whether his investigation was a success or a failure.

Getting the Picture

As Brannan looked at the corpse and visually scanned the room, he tried to determine what happened. Without touching the body, he examined fingers, fingernails, arms, and legs. He was looking for any wounds that indicated the victim had fought her attacker. He carefully studied the knot on the cord that tied the victim's hands. It was a distinctive kind of bow. The cord appeared to be from an iron that lay on the carpet beside the body. Brannan looked at the sheet covering the body. And he began to draw preliminary conclusions. The killer had struck quickly, probably smashing the victim's head with the iron.

There had been no time for Salazar to fight back. She was tied up and strangled. Then the sheet was placed over her by the killer. Brannan believed it meant that the killer did not want to have to look at the dead body. Perhaps the killer was bothered by the sight because he or she knew the victim.

Brannan's inspection of the apartment revealed no signs of forced entry—no broken windows, jimmied locks, or splintered door or window frames. He thought this was another sign that the victim knew her killer. She had let him or her in, or at least opened the door.

As the detective looked around the living room, he tried hard not to miss anything of significance. He looked for anything that seemed out of place or that might be evidence. He noticed a spot of blood on the carpet and a cigarette butt in an ashtray. He also looked for items that seemed to be missing. The telephone answering machine was gone. The stereo was missing, and CDs were strewn around on the floor. To make a complete list of everything that had been stolen from the apartment, he would interview the roommate, Jennifer Ledesma.

Directing the Team

When Supervisor Kratz arrived, Brannan informed him about what he had learned. As the homicide specialists arrived, both detectives supervised their activities. The medical examiner's office was in charge of removing the body so that it could be autopsied to determine the cause of death, but the detectives were in charge of everything else. The crime-scene photographers took pictures of everything that Brannan indicated, including the body and its position. Fingerprint specialists dusted for prints where Brannan directed. DNA evidence was gathered by lab technicians from spots Brannan chose. He also chose items of physical evidence that he wanted crime-scene investigators to collect for scientific testing, such as the cigarette butt.

Brannan drew his own sketch of the crime scene and continued to speak all his thoughts and discoveries into his tape recorder. He did not know if any of the physical evidence would

Homicide detectives point out where lab technicians should gather evidence.

eventually lead to a quick and easy solution of the case, but he had a bad feeling. Many homicide cases are easily solved, and a suspect is arrested within days. Solving Salazar's murder, however, looked as if it would not be so easy. His interviews with the roommate and responding officers suggested that she had not led the sort of dangerous or criminal lifestyle that so often resulted in murder. Brannan had a lot more work to do.

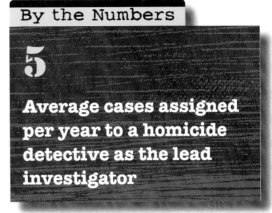

By the Numbers

5

Average cases assigned per year to a homicide detective as the lead investigator

Two Types of Homicides

Homicide detectives often distinguish between two types of homicides: Those that are easily solved and those that are mysteries, which take careful, extensive investigation to solve. Mysteries are cases with few clues about the perpetrator, no witnesses, and in which the motive is obscure. Brannan's case was a mystery, and that made it unusual. Cases that are easily solved are the most common. Some detectives call these cases slam dunks or "dunkers." Sometimes right at the crime scene or within a matter of minutes or hours, the detective identifies a suspect and knows who committed the homicide. Witnesses, for example, can make the detective's job very straightforward, even if they are reluctant witnesses.

Thomas McKenna was a New York City homicide detective. One evening he responded to a homicide call in which two people had been shot in the street. When he arrived on the scene, one victim lay dead in the street; the other had been taken to the hospital with a wounded arm. McKenna examined the crime scene and then went to the hospital to interview the second victim, Glen Allen. Allen insisted that he had seen nothing and knew nothing. He did not know his companion's name. He only knew his street nickname, "Bee." McKenna says, "I asked him just how good a friend of his Bee was. He said he was his best friend—his best friend, whose name he didn't know. I said 'Well, I've got to find out who he was, because we've got to notify his next of kin. He's dead.'"[4]

Allen did not know his friend had died and suddenly became very upset. He told McKenna, "Lonnie did it." McKenna asked why and Allen said, "Well, maybe Bee did something." Allen also told McKenna where Lonnie lived. After further investigation, McKenna discovered that the killing was about stealing drugs. It took a couple of days before he was able to a find and arrest Lonnie. McKenna says, "Only an hour and a half after we got the first report of the shooting, I had the name and address of a suspect, which wasn't bad progress."[5]

Luck Plus Talent

McKenna's case required that the detective use his interview skills, but it did not demand much investigation at the crime scene. He was also lucky, as detectives often say they have to be, that the second shooting victim was alive and able to describe what happened. The case was a dunker for McKenna.

One Baltimore, Maryland, homicide detective, however, had to use his observation skills at the crime scene to solve his case. Detective Donald Worden and his partner were called to an apartment in a rough part of town, where a man lay dead in his bed. He had been stabbed. While his partner examined the bedroom, Worden searched the rest of the apartment, looking for anything that seemed out of the ordinary. In the kitchen he discovered a sink full of dirty water. When he reached in and pulled the plug, he found a knife with a broken blade. Then Worden's eyes wandered down the kitchen counter. He saw a pile of dirty, unwashed dishes, drinking glasses, knives, forks, and spoons. Separate from this pile was one drinking glass.

Worden wondered if the killer had stopped to have a drink of water when he threw the knife into the sink. He called over the crime-scene technician and told him to check that glass for fingerprints. Later the fingerprints lifted from that glass were compared to the computer data bank of fingerprints at

Detective Donald Worden used fingerprints found on a glass at a crime scene to identify a killer.

Just a Face in the Crowd

When a murder occurred on a street in a Hispanic neighborhood in New York, several detectives responded to the scene, attracting a crowd of onlookers. As the lead detective took charge of the crime scene, one Puerto Rican detective, who spoke Spanish, melted into the crowd to listen to the talk. He was dressed in plainclothes, and no one realized he was a detective. Two men were discussing the murder. One remarked to the other in Spanish, "Hey, look over there, that guy has some nerve. First he kills the dude, and then he comes back with all these cops standing around just to look at the body." The detective quietly let the other detectives know what he had heard. The detectives suddenly rushed into the crowd and arrested the suspect. The watching man said, "Wow, those detectives are really smart. How did they know he killed that man?" Detectives never know what conversation at the crime scene may lead them to a killer. The Puerto Rican detective's alertness and attention solved a crime in which almost everyone might have refused to cooperate as a witness.

Quoted in Vernon J. Geberth, *Practical Homicide Investigation*, Boca Raton, FL: CRC Press, 1996, pp. 82–83.

the crime lab. The technicians found a match. It led Worden and his partner to the killer, a man with a long record of previous crimes. A murder that could have gone unsolved became a dunker because of Worden's detective skills and his careful observations at the crime scene.

Experienced Guesses

Sometimes, however, the most careful and conscientious crime-scene investigation is not enough. At a crime scene a homicide detective is often only beginning an investigation that may extend for days, weeks, or even years. He or she may find little obvious physical evidence at the crime scene, so the good homicide detective begins to formulate ideas about what may have happened. The goal at this stage is not limited to finding evidence that will be acceptable in court. It is also to find hints about who may have committed the crime.

A detective remains open to any and all possibilities. He or she does not want any murder to go unsolved because something was overlooked at the crime scene. Detectives often say that there are three things that solve crimes: physical evidence, witnesses, and confessions. According to crime writer David Simon in his book, *Homicide: A Year on the Killing Streets*, "A detective gets only one chance at a scene. You do what you do, and then the yellow plastic police-line-do-not-cross strips come down. [When the murder happens on a street,] the fire department turns a hose on the bloodstains; the lab techs move on to the next call; the neighborhood reclaims another patch of pavement."[6] Most of the physical evidence will be found at the crime scene, and so homicide detectives will collect any items from the scene that may be related to the murder. Even trash from the street may be carefully collected on a detective's hunch. Any items collected are bagged; marked with time, date, and identifying information; and kept in the Police Department's evidence room. Even if the case remains unsolved for years, the evidence is saved in case it can be of use in the future.

The Murder Notebook

Deciding what is evidence and leading the crime-scene team are large parts of a homicide detective's job, but they are not all that must be done. According to Geberth, "the homicide detective faces a monumental task at the crime scene."[7] Everything he or she does must be according to legal procedure and well-documented so that it can be used in court when a suspect goes to trial. Geberth developed an investigative procedure called the investigative checklist for detectives. It is a general outline of steps that new

Crime scene photographers are an essential part of thoroughly documenting a crime scene.

homicide detectives are taught to help ensure that a perpetrator is brought to justice. Detective training almost always includes studying and memorizing an investigation checklist. Everything on the checklist must be documented in the detective's notebook. Some of the events that must be recorded include:

Arriving at the Scene

Upon his or her arrival at a crime scene, a homicide detective writes down the exact time he or she arrived, the address, the weather and temperature conditions, and the people present. He or she notes the names and times of arrival of the responding officers and records what these officers did to preserve the crime scene. Without these facts, a defense attorney might be able to argue in court that the crime scene was contaminated by onlookers.

21

Performing a Preliminary Inspection

Next, a homicide detective tries to determine the name, address, sex, age, and race of the victim and records the information in the notebook. Although only a medical examiner can declare someone dead, the detective must still check and confirm that the victim is dead prior to the medical examiner's arrival. Most experienced detectives recognize death by body posture, lack of respiration, lack of a pulse, or wounds. If there is any doubt, the detective will call for medical assistance immediately. He or she then records the exact location of the body and describes the body and the scene. If the detective is successful in discovering the name of the victim, he or she orders a background check. This means running the victim's name through a computer review at police headquarters in order to search for any records of arrests, warrants, or convictions. If the detective learns, for example, that the victim is a known drug user or has a criminal record, this information may lead to a motive for the crime or even to criminal associates.

Initiating a Crime-Scene Log

A homicide detective assigns to one of the police officers at the scene the task of creating a crime-scene log. The officer must write down the name of every person at the scene, including civilians, police officers, emergency medical personnel, the medical examiner, crime-scene technicians, crime photographers, and any other professionals responding to the scene. The officer also records the arrival and departure time of each person. Again, these details ensure that police can accurately report in court that the scene was not contaminated by anyone who should not have had access. If just one time is recorded incorrectly, a good defense attorney may argue that all of the detective's other evidence is inaccurate, too.

Establishing Crime-Scene Integrity

A homicide detective is also responsible for documenting that the scene is protected from contamination and for recording anything that changes the crime scene. For example, responding officers or emergency personnel may have had to turn on lights in order to see the body. If this occurred, the detective must record that light switches were touched and are in the "on" positions because first responders had to turn on the lights. If emergency personnel tried to revive the victim, they may have pushed a piece of furniture out of the way or moved the body. These events, too, must be recorded in the detective's notebook.

Then the detective must be able to prove that no other changes were allowed to occur. Doors and windows must be documented as open or closed. Telephones must be protected and not touched. No facilities at the scene, such as toilets or faucets, may be used.

The detective also must check and write down the conditions of appliances (off or on), lamps, televisions, radios, computers, clocks, and beepers. The detective will write down the last date a computer was used and check beeper messages. With voice mail or beeper messages, he or she will record the messages and save the recordings as evidence.

Initiating a Canvass

Either personally or by directing other officers, a detective searches the area of the crime scene for witnesses or anyone who may know anything about the homicide. If police are knocking on doors, they must write down each address, the number of people inside, their names, and what each person said. All automobiles in the area are also documented, along with their license-plate numbers. Detectives do this because sometimes the killer, or people with knowledge of the killer, lingers at the scene of the crime to watch the investigation.

Photographing the Crime Scene

A homicide detective ensures that photographs are discretely taken of any onlookers at the crime scene. Photos are also taken of the crime scene itself and of the surrounding area. Photos of

Becoming a Homicide Detective

Job Description:
As a member of law enforcement, a homicide detective conducts an investigation of a murder with the goal of identifying and apprehending the killer and achieving justice for the victim and the survivors. The investigator is responsible for gathering facts and evidence that will lead to successful prosecution of the killer in a court of law.

Education:
The job of homicide detective always requires a minimum of a high school education, but may require a two-year associate's degree, or a four-year college degree, depending on the Police Department. A college degree is recommended. Some suggested majors include criminal justice, police science, public administration, criminology, forensics, and law enforcement.

Qualifications:
An applicant must have worked as a police officer for a certain period of time, usually at least two to three years, before becoming eligible to advance to detective. On-the-job experience and training are the most important qualifications for a promotion to detective. An officer is appointed to a detective squad by its commanding officer based on his or her experience, abilities, and arrest record. Occasionally an officer will be asked to take a written test. A new detective usually works on investigations of lesser crimes in a detective division, such as robbery, narcotics, or juvenile crimes. After one or two years of experience in these areas, he or she becomes eligible to be considered for detective in the Homicide Division. A supervisor or chief of the Homicide Division or Homicide Squad will conduct an interview with the detective and decide whether to make the appointment.

Additional Information:
Traits considered most important for the job of homicide detective include interrogation and interviewing skills, dedication, patience, experience,

common sense, persistence, and organizational abilities. In addition, a detective must be able to accurately fill out reports and keep records. A new homicide detective is paired with an experienced detective in order to learn investigative skills in the field. Commonly, the new detective will not be the lead, or primary, detective on a homicide case until he or she has worked with an experienced detective for several investigations and is deemed ready to control an investigation by his or her partner and the supervisor of the squad.

Salary:
$35,000 to $95,000 per year

witnesses and the victim are taken. If a witness has any injuries or marks on their clothing (that could be blood or rips from a fight), these are photographed as well. For each photograph, the detective records the date and time it was taken, the exact location it was taken, light and weather conditions, a description of the photograph, and the name of the person taking the photograph.

Sketching the Crime Scene

A homicide detective is also responsible for drawing a sketch of the crime scene that includes a stick figure representing the body, the room or place where the body lies, and any furniture or objects at the scene. On the sketch, the detective has to include measurements, such as the distance from the body to a door or bed. He or she must also note the compass direction of the victim's head, such as north, south, east, or west.

Searching the Crime Scene

A homicide detective tries to reconstruct in his or her mind what happened at a crime scene. He or she tries to determine the killer's point of entry and escape route, as well as what the weapon might be and where it is located. Then, using only his or her eyes, a detective visually decides what should be gathered as evidence, what should be tested for fingerprints or DNA, and what other areas should be searched for clues. All gathered evidence is written down.

Processing Evidence

A homicide detective must establish a chain of custody for all evidence collected. This means documenting the name of the detective or crime-scene technician who actually collects each piece of evidence. It means recording exactly where the evidence was at the scene and the time it was collected. All the evidence is photographed and placed in a package or bag so that it remains uncontaminated. Whenever anyone takes possession of the evidence, he or she must document that it was handed over, to whom it was given, and that it remained sealed.

Just the Beginning

Only after these and other procedures are completed and documented can a homicide detective leave the crime scene. Often police are finished working a crime scene in a few hours, but sometimes, it may be maintained for several days so that detectives can return, if necessary. Usually a careful investigation that follows an investigative checklist solves the homicide, but not always. Sometimes the initial investigation yields little in the way of evidence, and the identity of the killer remains unknown. No detective wants a case to remain unsolved, so the homicide investigation continues beyond the crime scene until an arrest can be made.

CHAPTER 2

Making a Case

After the initial crime-scene investigation is complete, the legwork and chasing down of leads begin. A homicide detective has to wait for results from crime labs on evidence, such as fingerprints, DNA, and bloodstains. But there may be evidence among friends and family, too. No two homicide cases are alike, so a detective has to be flexible and follow up on every possibility. He or she is looking for witnesses, confessions, and physical evidence. Detectives will try to find good witnesses with information, even when that information is just gossip. They will identify suspects and hope for a confession. And they use evidence gathered at the crime scene to verify the information that they gather. A detective has to carefully compile and compare all the data before he or she can achieve the desired result—an arrest.

Working with the Medical Examiner

The physical evidence from the crime scene is critical to solving a case, and the body of the victim is the most important source of physical evidence. For this reason, homicide detectives usually have close working relationships with medical examiners. Detectives will often attend the autopsy and obtain information from the medical examiner. The knowledge gained during the autopsy can help in all the subsequent stages of the homicide investigation.

It is the medical examiner who establishes the cause and manner of death. A medical examiner (ME) is a doctor who specializes in determining how someone died by dissecting and examining a body in a process called an autopsy. There are five possible manners of death: homicide, suicide, accident, natural, or unknown (for those cases in which an autopsy does not identify a reason). If the death is a homicide, the cause of death

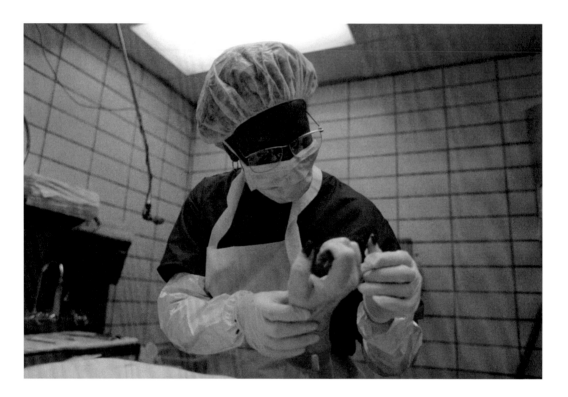

A medical examiner conducts an autopsy, an important part of a detective's case. may be a bullet or stab wound, poison, suffocation, blunt force trauma (such as being hit over the head), or any other violent action. Once the medical examiner rules the death a homicide, the homicide detective has the evidence of murder that will be needed in court.

The medical examiner may also discover important physical evidence during the autopsy that helps the detective build a case. Crime writer David Simon explains,

> Given a gunshot wound, a medical examiner can determine from the amount and pattern of soot, burned powder, and other debris whether a particular bullet was fired at contact range, close range, or a distance greater than two to two and a half feet.... From an exit wound, an ME can tell whether a victim was standing free or if the wound is shored because the victim was against a wall, or on a floor, or in a chair.... Give that same doctor a knife wound and you'll learn whether or not the blade

had one edge or two, was serrated or straight.... Then there are the blunt trauma injuries: Was your victim hit by a car or a lead pipe? Did that infant fall in the bathtub or was he bludgeoned by the babysitter? In either case [the medical examiner] has the key.[8]

The detective attends the autopsy with the murder notebook and records all of the medical examiner's findings, as well as documenting any evidence removed for testing, such as bullets or dirt from a wound or hairs on the clothing of the body. The notes are evidence if the case goes to trial and show that a bullet, for instance, did indeed come from the body of the victim and not from some other place. The evidence acquired from the body during an autopsy can provide the clues that help a detective solve a case.

Using Autopsy Evidence

Baltimore, Maryland, homicide detective Harry Edgerton used autopsy evidence to find a killer and build a case against him. Edgerton's case was the murder of twelve-year-old Andrea Perry. She had been shot in the head, and her body was dumped

A firearms examiner can determine whether a gun found by detectives is the murder weapon.

in an alley. At the autopsy, which Edgerton observed, the medical examiner removed a .32-caliber bullet from Perry's skull. He also found semen in the body that proved the girl had been sexually molested. Edgerton did not have a suspect, but he was determined to catch this killer. On a hunch, he notified police stations in three districts in the area to let him know immediately if they had any crimes that involved a .32-caliber gun and sexual assault.

Manner of Death: Unknown

A medical examiner is not always able to determine if a death is a homicide, even when a detective is sure it is murder. When a woman, who was a known alcoholic, was found dead on a truck loading dock, Baltimore, Maryland, detectives Donald Worden and Dave Brown thought it was a homicide. The woman was covered with tread marks from truck tires. The detectives attended the medical examiner's autopsy. They believed the bruises on the victim's arms proved she had been grabbed. The medical examiner said they could have been caused when the truck hit her. The detectives pointed out torn clothes and earrings ripped from her ears, but the medical examiner said that also could have happened from being run over. The medical examiner found no cuts or bruises on the victim's legs. This indicated to her that the victim, who was determined to be drunk, was lying down in the lot and possibly passed out when she was hit. If she had been standing up, her legs would have been struck by the car, and some trauma would have been visible. The medical examiner said it easily could have been an accident. Brown and Worden believed that the alcoholic victim had been grabbed and murdered and that her body had been run over to hide the murder. But the medical examiner could not prove it with the autopsy. Without further evidence, the medical examiner had to determine the manner of death as unknown.

Two weeks after he made that request, a report came in. A thirteen-year-old girl had been raped. The rapist had threatened her with a "silver-looking" handgun. He had said he would shoot her "in the back of the head"[9] if she told anyone. The girl ran home and told her mother what happened anyway. She recognized the man who attacked her; he was the boyfriend of her best friend's mother. The police were called, and they immediately called the homicide division to report the crime. Edgerton's partner joined the officers who set out to arrest the man. Eugene Dale was not at home when they arrived, but officers searched his house and found a .32-caliber weapon in a linen closet.

Later that day, Dale was arrested by the patrol officers guarding his house. He was brought to the homicide squad so that Edgerton could question him. The gun had already been taken to the ballistics lab, where the firearms examiner was testing it. Although Edgerton could not persuade Dale to confess, it did not matter. The firearms examiner compared a bullet fired from the gun in the lab to the bullet retrieved from Andrea Perry's body during the autopsy. They matched and that evidence was enough to charge Dale with first-degree murder.

The Best Physical Evidence

Even more evidence was collected during Andrea Perry's autopsy. By the time Dale was arrested, the semen found in Perry's body had been sent for DNA testing. DNA is the genetic blueprint in the cells of every living thing. DNA determines how each living thing grows and develops. It is unique to each individual. In a DNA laboratory, scientists can determine a person's DNA from a sample of body fluid, such as saliva or semen. Then they can compare samples of DNA and tell if they came from the same person. In Andrea Perry's case, the semen that the medical examiner found in her body during the autopsy was sent to a DNA laboratory. Edgerton's job was to find another sample to compare it with. For that,

Becoming a Police Officer

Job Description:
A police officer's job is to protect life and property in a variety of ways. They include patrolling an assigned area, issuing citations and warnings to those who break the law, investigating suspicious activities, apprehending and arresting suspected criminals, responding to calls for assistance, and maintaining peace and order in the community. A uniformed police officer may also be responsible for directing traffic at an accident scene, investigating a burglary, or giving first aid to an injured citizen.

Education:
The minimum educational requirement is a high school diploma, but a two-year associate's degree or a four-year college degree is recommended. If the officer wants to advance in the department, having a higher education is important. Those officers who make detective, sergeant, lieutenant, chief, or supervisor, for example, have acquired both education and experience.

Qualifications:
Once accepted by a Police Department, most new recruits must receive twelve to fourteen weeks of training in a police academy. In addition to graduating from the police academy, officers must meet rigorous physical and psychological standards. Candidates have to pass physical examinations for vision, hearing, and strength. They must pass a drug test and are often required to take lie-detector tests. Sometimes they are examined by a psychologist or given a personality test to ensure that they are honest, responsible, and of sound judgment. In most states, officers also must be U.S. citizens and at least twenty years old.

Additional Information:
A police officer must like working with the public and be willing to work long hours when necessary. Whether on duty or off duty, a police officer is expected to remain armed at all times and to use his or her authority whenever it is necessary to maintain public safety.

Salary:
Salary: $35,600 to $72,450 per year

he needed a suspect. When DNA testing is performed accurately and carefully by DNA experts, the chances that two matching DNA samples came from different individuals are less than one in one trillion—greater than the human population on Earth. DNA, therefore, is the best physical evidence a homicide detective can have.

A Search Warrant for DNA

Once Dale was in jail, Edgerton's bullet evidence and the thirteen-year-old girl's identification were enough for him to get a special search warrant. A search warrant is a legal authorization for police officers and detectives to perform a search for evidence. A detective cannot search someone's home or property without a search warrant. To get a search warrant, a detective fills out an affidavit, a sworn statement, describing the reasons why police want permission to search. These reasons are called probable cause. A judge reads the affidavit,

Detective Edgerton was able to get a warrant to take some of Dale's blood for DNA evidence.

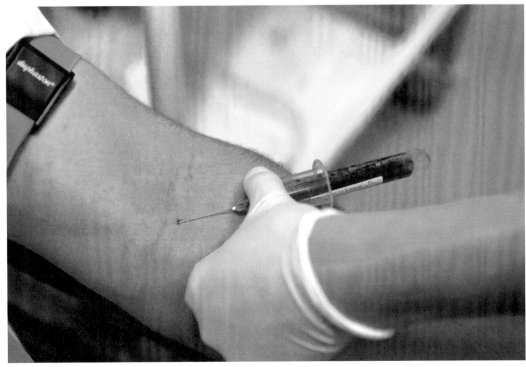

By the Numbers

25

Number of states that require the permanent preservation of DNA evidence in criminal cases

and if he or she agrees that there is reasonable cause to believe a suspect has committed a crime, then the judge will give permission, in the form of a search warrant, for the search.

Edgerton wanted to search Dale's body for evidence, not his house or car. He wanted a DNA sample to compare to the sample taken from Perry's body. His search warrant gave him permission to collect samples of Dale's blood and hair. (Today DNA warrants are usually for saliva, but when Edgerton was investigating this homicide in 1988, DNA labs were most accurate with blood and hair samples.) The warrant was signed by a judge who agreed that Edgerton had probable cause to demand the sample.

Dale was not happy with the demand; he claimed that someone had borrowed his gun and murdered the girl. He told Edgerton, "I don't want to…. I want to talk to a lawyer." Edgerton, who was outraged by the crime Dale had committed, was not polite with his response. He answered, "Either you let [the nurse] take some blood and some hairs the easy way or I'm going to take it myself, because the warrant says I can. And I can tell you that you'd definitely rather have her do it."[10] Dale finally agreed to cooperate. Later the DNA lab matched his samples with the one taken from Perry's body. Dale was tried and convicted for Andrea Perry's murder and sentenced to life in prison without parole. For Edgerton, the result was a source of deep satisfaction.

When DNA Cannot Help

Detective Curt Brannan was not as lucky with the semen sample that the medical examiner found in Brenda Salazar's body. The lab was able to get DNA from the sample, but Brannan could find no suspect for comparison. The same

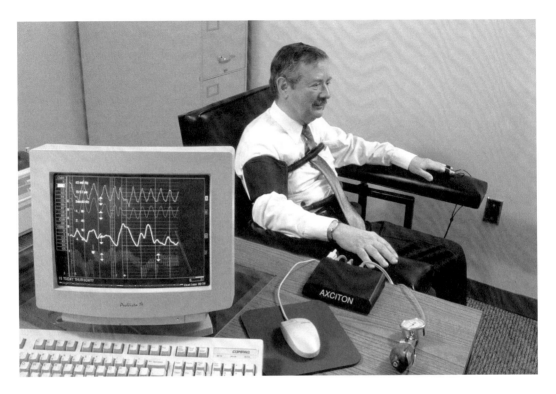

thing happened with a fingerprint that was lifted from Salazar's abandoned car. The evidence was saved, but it did not help in the investigation. Until Brannan found a suspect, the physical evidence was useless to him. He had to work on his investigation the old-fashioned way—with legwork and a hope for some lucky breaks. He interviewed Salazar's parents and sister, trying to find out everything they knew about her life, her friends, and any boyfriends. The sister, Rosalia, remembered Salazar mentioning a man named Tommy from her work. He had once playfully wrapped his hands around her neck. He had kissed her without permission. Brannan followed up on the lead.

Brannan went to the telemarketing company where Salazar had worked and found the Tommy who worked there. Tommy agreed to come to the detective's office for questioning. He agreed to take a polygraph, or lie detector, test. Detectives often depend on polygraph testing to help them identify and eliminate suspects. Many detectives

Polygraph results cannot be used in court but can help steer detectives in the right direction.

35

Polygraph Testing

Polygraphs do not actually identify lies. They measure a person's stress levels from the emotional changes that occur when someone is nervous. A qualified polygraph examiner uses a polygraph machine that tests for physiological, or bodily, changes that typically occur when someone answers questions deceptively or untruthfully. The theory is that everyone is at least a little nervous when lying. The test works this way:

1 The examiner sits alone in a room with the subject to be questioned and the medical polygraph equipment.

2 Two air-filled rubber tubes are placed around the subject's chest and abdomen. They are attached to the examiner's computerized polygraph equipment and measure respirations (breaths) per minute.

3 A blood pressure cuff is placed around the subject's upper arm. The cuff is connected to the polygraph by tubes that convert changes in blood pressure to electrical signals.

4 Two finger plates, called galvanometers, are connected to the subject's fingertips. They measure galvanic skin response, which is a measure of sweat or the electrical conductivity of the skin. (Wet skin conducts electricity more easily that dry skin.)

5 The examiner conducts an interview or pretest with the subject. The examiner explains the test, and the subject tells his or her side of the story about the crime under investigation. Through many questions, the examiner establishes a baseline of the subject's physiological responses. The examiner can see how nervous the subject is in general and how he or she reacts to questions. Some questions are repeated several times, in different ways, to be sure about the levels of stress attached to those questions. The examiner asks specific questions about the crime and prepares the subject by going over what they will be.

6 The formal test is administered. It consists of about eleven questions, but only three or four of them are about the crime. The others are called control questions and establish a baseline for the subject's stress levels. For example, when asked what he or she ate for breakfast, the subject's breathing, heart, and sweat levels may remain normal. When asked about the crime, the subject's heart rate, breathing, and sweating may increase if a lie is told or the truth is evaded. When telling an obvious lie, such as answering "no" when asked whether you have ever told a fib in your life, the changes in the subject's body tell the examiner the subject's typical stress levels during deception.

7 The examiner analyzes the results. He or she then determines whether the subject tested as deceptive or truthful about the crime. Experts say the accuracy of this determination may be anywhere between 70 percent and 90 percent, but it is not 100 percent accurate for all subjects. A false positive result means that the examiner determined the subject to be deceptive when he or she was actually truthful. This can happen with very frightened people. A false negative means that a deceptive subject is determined by the examiner to be telling the truth. Some subjects try to beat polygraph testing by putting deodorant on their fingers or wearing a tack inside a shoe. They have dry fingers and step on the tack when answering any question, thus increasing their stress levels as they increase pain levels.

believe that refusing to take a polygraph test makes a person suspicious and that he or she probably has something to hide. Polygraph test results, however, cannot be used in court. The courts have ruled that such testing is not accurate enough to be trusted, and they will not accept the test results as evidence. Tommy, however, passed the

By the Numbers

2

Hours needed for a properly conducted polygraph test

polygraph test. When questioned about Salazar's death, his answers tested as truthful when he insisted he knew nothing.

Brannan interviewed all of Salazar's friends and acquaintances. Any time he got another name, he checked out that person. Even if Salazar had dated a man only once, Brannan still checked out the man. He went to the restaurant where Salazar had held a part-time job. He interviewed everyone there. He went to the school where she had been taking classes. He interviewed men who were in the same classes. He even asked male friends and acquaintances to volunteer to give blood samples for DNA testing, in order to rule them out as suspects. He had nowhere near enough probable cause to get a search warrant to force the men to give samples, but many of the men agreed anyway. They wanted Brannan to be able to eliminate them as suspects in order to help find Salazar's killer. No one matched the sample taken from Salazar's body. Brannan talked to dozens of people, but he found no one who might be a suspect. By September 1997, four months after Salazar's murder, Brannan had run out of leads to follow. Although he would not give up, there was nothing left for him to investigate.

Detectives do not always solve their homicide cases, and Brannan hoped that this would not be one of those unsolved homicides. He assured Salazar's mother, "This case will not be forgotten. It's not going to be put in a drawer, Mrs. Salazar, and forgotten as long as I'm a detective in this unit.... I know [the case] and anything that comes in, I will compare to this case, any other similar cases. Sometimes people start talking; information comes in with a phone call and all of a sudden it cracks ... wide open."[11] All Brannan could do now was wait and hope for some luck or perhaps an anonymous phone tip.

People Will Talk

Phone tips do help solve cases, but detectives have to use their experience to analyze the practical value of tips. Many anonymous tips are like crank phone calls or are from people who are trying to cause trouble. Other tipsters give their names and want to help police but still actually know nothing. Sometimes they are people who have mental or emotional problems. Sometimes they are people who believe they have psychic powers. Sometimes they are just people who are excited to have a reason to call police. For that reason, detectives usually do not allow some of the crime scene evidence to become public knowledge. They will keep some key piece of information confidential, so that they will know whether a tipster's statements are credible, or believable. This tactic does not work all the time, but it helps to weed out truly worthless tips and saves detectives a lot of work. A good tip, however, can start detectives down a trail that leads to a killer.

A Good Phone Tip

On the night of January 16, 1997, Ennis Cosby, the son of actor and comedian Bill Cosby, was killed. The twenty-seven-year-old man was found lying beside his Mercedes on the shoulder of a Los Angeles, California, freeway. He had been changing a flat tire when he was shot in the head. In Los Angeles, very difficult murder investigations or murders that involve high-profile or famous people are handled by a homicide division known as Homicide Special. This is an elite detective squad, made up of the best, most-experienced homicide detectives. The murder of Bill Cosby's son caused a lot of media coverage and yet was a tough case to solve. There were no immediate suspects and no obvious motives for the murder. Detective John Garcia of Homicide Special was assigned the Cosby investigation.

When Garcia arrived at the crime scene, Cosby still lay beside the car with a pack of cigarettes in his hand. There was cash in his pocket, and an expensive watch on his wrist.

An anonymous tip led detectives to suspect Mikail Markhasev, who was convicted of the Cosby murder.

It appeared to Garcia that Cosby had been surprised by his attacker and was shot without warning. Robbery did not seem to be the motive, but Garcia could not be sure. He did have a witness, a friend of Cosby's named Stephanie Crane. She had received a phone call from Cosby when he got the flat tire. He had asked her to drive over and shine her car's headlights on his car so he could see to change the tire. When Garcia interviewed Crane, she told him about a very pale-looking man who came up to her car in the darkness. The man yelled at her, "Get out of the car or I'll kill you."[12] She did not get out; she drove away.

Then, she said, when she turned around to see where the man went, Cosby was lying on the ground by his car, and the man was running away.

Garcia asked Crane for a detailed description of the killer. He speculated that the killer may have been a drug addict (because of his very pale complexion) who meant to rob Cosby for money but panicked and ran away. Later Garcia got a police artist to draw a picture of the suspect from Crane's description and had it published in the news. Hundreds of leads and tips came into Homicide Special. Garcia and a team of detectives followed up on every credible lead. They interviewed the tipsters and interviewed the people that the tipsters had named. It took a lot of work to follow all these leads. The detectives went all over the city to talk to hundreds of people, but none of the tips led to a break in the case. Reporters began to criticize Garcia and his investigative skills. But with no solid leads, he could do nothing.

Then two months after the murder, an anonymous tip changed everything. The tipster asked if Cosby had been killed with a .38-caliber bullet. This was a critical piece of information that the detectives had kept from the media. The tipster had not given his name, but he had left his beeper number. Garcia tracked the man down through his pager company and personally interviewed him to find out what he knew. The man told Garcia about two young male acquaintances, an Asian teenager (whose name the caller knew) and a Russian (whom he did not know). The two had asked him for a ride one night. They made him stop at a rest stop on the freeway, went into the brush by the side of the road, and then returned a few minutes later. He heard the Russian say he had killed someone. And the Asian told him that they had been searching the brush for the gun that the Russian had thrown there in a panic. They wanted to find it and bury it somewhere else. The tipster may not have known the Russian's name, but he did know that both young men were criminals and had been cell mates in juvenile prison. Garcia first called in a group of police officers to search the brush by the rest stop. The search team found the gun—it was a .38 caliber—hidden under a brown stocking cap. The cap was bagged for DNA testing. The gun was taken for testing by the firearms expert. DNA was obtained from hairs stuck in the cap, and the gun proved to be the same one that had been used to kill Cosby. Before this physical evidence could be of any use, however, Garcia had to find the Russian. He got a name by looking up juvenile prison records. In prisons, the names of all prisoners and their cell assignments, past and present, are kept on file. Garcia checked the records for the name of the Asian's cell mate. The young man was not Russian, but Ukrainian, and his name was Mikail Markhasev.

Finding Markhasev was not easy, but a citywide search by a team of detectives finally led to his arrest. He insisted he was innocent of the crime, but Garcia's investigation uncovered more evidence against him. The Asian, Michael Chang, was a

Death Notification

Usually it is a homicide detective's job to notify a victim's family members of the death. It is a painful part of the detective's job. Family members are the secondary victims of a homicide. Detectives know that family members are facing a horrifying circumstance and terrible grief when a loved one is murdered. The detective must tell family members about the death, express sympathy for their loss, help them go to the morgue to identify the victim, interview them as part of the investigation, and support them as they cope with the courts and the legal system. If a family member is a suspect, a detective must be respectful even when he or she is suspicious and seeking information. A detective knows that other family members are still victims. For most detectives, finding the murderer and bringing him or her to justice is not only a serious responsibility but also the best thing they can do for the survivors.

reluctant witness, but he did tell Garcia that Markhasev admitted to killing someone and that it was "all over the news."[13] Garcia then tracked down other friends of Markhasev at a house on Mulholland Drive. Markhasev had been at their house drinking and using cocaine on the night of the murder, along with two other friends. Garcia found and interviewed those friends. They admitted to Garcia that they left with Markhasev that night, planning to drive to a dealer's house and steal his drugs. When Markhasev spotted Cosby's expensive car along the way, he told them, "I'm going to jack [rob] that guy." The friends waited in the car. When Markhasev returned to the car, he said, "Let's get … out of here. I just shot the guy. He didn't move fast enough."[14] With witnesses describing Markhasev's own admissions, DNA evidence, and the gun, Garcia had a solid case. His investigation had successfully identified a killer.

Difficult, But Worth It

Although the original anonymous tip had been a starting point in Garcia's investigation, it was his investigative skill that led him to Cosby's murderer. When he found and persuaded Markhasev's friends to talk, he was following leads and then using the interviews and bits of information to learn the truth.

Detective Thomas McKenna explains, "An investigation is a matter of a lot of hard work, canvassing a neighborhood, talking to maybe hundreds of witnesses or potential witnesses, gathering information, gathering facts. It's a matter of little things making a big thing and making a successful prosecution."[15] A successful prosecution is the ultimate goal for a homicide detective, and Garcia achieved that goal. Markhasev was sentenced to life in prison without the possibility of parole on August 11, 1998. Bill Cosby telephoned Garcia personally and thanked him for catching his son's murderer.

CHAPTER 3

Interrogations and Arrests

People talk to their friends. They talk to their families and girlfriends or boyfriends. They gossip about the rumors they have heard. Sometimes they brag about their deeds. In an interrogation room, however, people rarely want to tell a homicide detective the truth. Detectives have a saying: "Everyone lies."[16] A homicide detective cannot beat the truth out of a witness or suspect. The detective cannot threaten violence. So, the best homicide detectives use psychological tactics and tricks to get the information they need. Sometimes they get a critical piece of information. Sometimes they get a confession. Often, they get lies, but even lies can further an investigation. It all depends on the skills of the detective.

Gunned Down in the Street

On a dark winter night in Baltimore, Maryland, police officer Gene Cassidy got out of his squad car and pushed his way into a crowd of young people loitering on a street corner. He had spotted a drug dealer, Butchie Frazier, who had an outstanding arrest warrant. Cassidy called out to the man, "Hey, I want to talk to you. Put your hands against the wall."[17] Frazier pretended to obey and then pulled a handgun from his pocket. Cassidy had no time to reach for his own gun. Frazier shot Cassidy twice in the left side of the head. Cassidy fell to the ground, and the crowd of people ran away.

Another officer discovered Cassidy on the sidewalk a few minutes later. An ambulance rushed Cassidy to a hospital, but he was not expected to survive. His face and head were a bloody, unrecognizable mess. Homicide detective Terry McLarney was assigned to the case. There were plenty of witnesses, but no one would admit to having seen anything. No one would name Frazier as the shooter.

After weeks in the hospital, Cassidy did survive, but he was left blind and completely unable to remember anything about that terrible night. He could not help with the case. After three months of investigating and talking to people on the street, McLarney finally got a few names of people who were there when Cassidy was shot, and those people (who said they knew nothing) gave him more names so he would leave them alone. McLarney heard a rumor that Frazier was involved in the shooting. He had a hunch that the rumor about Frazier was true, but he could not prove it. McLarney kept asking questions and looking for more witnesses. Eventually he got the name of Yolanda Marks, Frazier's girlfriend.

A Witness Interrogation

Seventeen-year-old Yolanda and her mother were brought to the Police Department. Yolanda was not under arrest or even a suspect, but detectives had to find out what she knew. Her mother came with her because it is illegal for police to question anyone under eighteen years old unless a parent is present. Yolanda insisted she knew nothing. McLarney pressured the teen by telling her about Officer Cassidy's blindness. He described what it would be like to live in perpetual darkness. He told her that Cassidy's wife was pregnant, and that he would never see his new baby. McLarney then appealed to Yolanda's emotions by talking about morality and good versus evil until she broke down crying. "Think about those things," he said, and then he left her alone for a few minutes. When McLarney left, her mother encouraged her to tell the truth. She told her daughter to "get it over with and do the right thing."[18]

Yolanda sobbed because she loved Frazier. She did not want to tell the truth, but the relentless pressure in that small, bare interrogation room was too much for her. Finally she told McLarney that she had been on the corner with Frazier. She

45

Interrogation, or interview, rooms are often completely bare to intensify the pressure on the interviewee.

admitted, "Butchie shot the police."[19] Later she took a polygraph test that indicated she was telling the truth.

McLarney got justice for Cassidy and solved his case because of his interrogation of Yolanda. His appeal that Yolanda do the right thing and tell the truth worked because she was not a criminal herself. This approach, however, rarely works with witnesses who are criminals themselves. Former New York homicide detective Vernon J. Geberth says that often a detective has to "look for any weaknesses or fears" that can be used against the witness. "Usually these types [of people] are not too anxious to have police probing into their life style and may be willing to cooperate either for a price or just to 'get the cops off their back.' Sometimes you may be lucky enough to have something on them, such as a lesser crime, which can be traded off for information on the homicide,"[20] explains Geberth.

Using Weaknesses

Detective Thomas McKenna investigated the murder of Kim Stapleton in New York in 1990. She was the sister of actress Jean Stapleton, who is best known for her role as Edith Bunker on the 1970s television show *All in the Family*. Kim Stapleton had been standing on a street corner when a car stopped beside her, and someone reached out to snatch her purse. Unable to free herself from the purse strap, Stapleton was dragged to her death as the car sped off. While he was investigating the case, McKenna received a phone call from one of the police

Dying Declaration

In court a witness may not repeat what they heard someone else say. This is called hearsay and it is not admissible. An exception to this rule is the dying declaration, the final words and statement of a dying person. When Carlton Robinson was shot on the streets of Baltimore, Maryland, the first officer on the scene found him still alive and asked who shot him. Robinson said a coworker named Warren Waddell had shot him. The officer told the responding detectives, "Yeah, he said his buddy Warren shot him in the back for no reason. He kept saying, 'I can't believe he shot me. I can't believe it.'" These words would be admissible in court if Robinson knew he was dying and that death was imminent. In this case, the officer had not told Robinson he was dying, and Robinson had not stated that he was dying. During the ambulance ride to the hospital, however, the paramedics heard Robinson say that he knew he was dying. This was enough for his statements to the officer to be considered a dying declaration. The officer was allowed to testify to the declaration in court, and Waddell was convicted of murder.

Quoted in David Simon, *Homicide: A Year on the Killing Streets*, Boston, MA: Houghton Mifflin, 1991, p. 513.

precincts. A woman named Millie Salas had been arrested for drug use and was being held at the jail. Hoping to get the charges against her dropped, Salas claimed she had information about Stapleton's murder. She not only provided information about the man who killed Stapleton, but Salas also spent time with the homicide detectives helping them find the places the man hung out so they could arrest him. The minor drug charges against Salas were dropped because she helped police.

In another case, McKenna and his partner, Chris Heimgartner, played on the fears of their reluctant witnesses. They were investigating a killing that was the result of a street fight between two young men. The investigation led to two teenage girls who had witnessed the fight. They did not want to give the detectives any information. McKenna says, "We told them we could hold them as accessories after the fact [people who illegally aid a criminal], that we would take them to the station house, that we would call their parents and so forth. I'm a bad guy. Basically, I browbeat those two girls. And they told us who the [suspect] was."[21]

One Admission at a Time

At other times, detectives persuade witnesses to talk by pretending to be sympathetic and understanding. McKenna used this approach with a very reluctant witness who was afraid to give information. The suspect was a violent crack dealer. He had shot someone who had stolen his drug money. McKenna was pretty sure the witness had seen the murder. He persuaded the witness to come to the station for an interview. McKenna explains how he leads a witness like this to open up:

> I have a step procedure I use in these cases. The first step is to get the witness to admit he heard the shot. If you can get him that far along, you have a live witness…. So you say to your witness, "Okay, you heard the shot, so you looked. You *had* to look. You wanted to get away from the shooter, whether he was shooting at you or not, so you had to look. You couldn't get away

from the shooter if you didn't know where he was. You looked, pal. So tell us what you saw."

The next thing you say is "I suppose you didn't see the guy fire the shot. No. You looked after you heard the shot. What you saw was the guy standing there with the gun in his hand. You can't testify that you saw the guy shoot the gun, and I'm not asking you to testify to that. Hey, I'm your friend. I wouldn't ask you to testify you saw the guy shoot the gun when you didn't. All I want you to say is what you saw, that the guy had the gun in his hand."

This is the way you work on a witness step by step. It's not a quick process. Sometimes it takes hours.... I did something else [with this witness].... I got him a Coke. Then he wanted another one. I got him another one. Over the hours, he drank about six Cokes. By the by he wanted to go to the bathroom. I said no, not until we get this settled....

Of course he got very uncomfortable. What I was saying to him at this point was, "Look, we know you didn't do anything wrong. You're not accused of anything. So give us this statement we need, and then you can go to the bathroom."[22]

McKenna's witness talked and admitted he had seen the suspect shoot the victim. Another homicide case was as good as solved. McKenna had an admitted eyewitness to the crime. Had this witness been a criminal suspect, McKenna never could have used discomfort to get the statement, since courts have ruled that such interrogation tactics are illegal. However, as a witness, his informant was not subject to the same legal protection. The witness's statement was sufficient evidence for an arrest in the murder case. Although reluctantly given, his testimony in court would help in the conviction, too.

Suspect Interrogation

A reluctant witness can be pressured in several ways, but if a person is a suspect, then detectives must be very careful about how they conduct the interrogation. Strict laws protect the rights of anyone accused of a crime. Even suspects who are not yet arrested cannot be coerced, or forced, in any way to answer questions or to make statements. For example, if McKenna's witness had been

DEFENDANT	LOCATION

SPECIFIC WARNING REGARDING INTERROGATIONS

1. YOU HAVE THE RIGHT TO REMAIN SILENT.

2. ANYTHING YOU SAY CAN AND WILL BE USED AGAINST YOU IN A COURT OF LAW.

3. YOU HAVE THE RIGHT TO TALK TO A LAWYER AND HAVE HIM PRESENT WITH YOU WHILE YOU ARE BEING QUESTIONED.

4. IF YOU CANNOT AFFORD TO HIRE A LAWYER ONE WILL BE APPOINTED TO REPRESENT YOU BEFORE ANY QUESTIONING, IF YOU WISH ONE.

SIGNATURE OF DEFENDANT	DATE
WITNESS	TIME

☐ REFUSED SIGNATURE   SAN FRANCISCO POLICE DEPARTMENT   PR.9.1.4

a suspect, he could not have refused to allow him to use the bathroom. That would be coercion. Any statements the suspect made could not have been used in court. Either the judge would have thrown them out as obtained illegally or the defense lawyer would have told the jury that the statements could not be trusted since they were made under unfair pressure.

Detectives operate under legal constraints whenever they speak to a suspect in a crime. First, all suspects must be given what is known as a Miranda warning and informed of their rights. Usually, the detective reads these rights to the suspect from a printed card, so that there can be no doubt that it was done correctly. Many detectives initial and save the card as evidence to be used in court. It is proof that the suspect was read his rights. The card reads:

Detectives usually read the Miranda warning from a card, informing the suspect of his or her rights.

MIRANDA WARNING

1. You have the right to remain silent.
2. Anything you say can and will be used against you in a court of law.

3. You have the right to talk to a lawyer and have him present with you while you are being questioned.

4. If you cannot afford to hire a lawyer, one will be appointed to represent you before any questioning, if you wish one.

WAIVER

After the warning and in order to secure a waiver, the following questions should be asked and an affirmative reply secured to each question:

1. Do you understand each of these rights I have explained to you?

2. Having these rights in mind, do you wish to talk to us now?[23]

Waiving Rights

After a detective reads a suspect his rights, he or she records in the murder notebook the time, date, location, and any witnesses. Then the detective tries to get the suspect to sign a Miranda waiver. If the suspect signs it, then it means that the

Homicide detectives often videotape their interrogations so they can be used as evidence at a trial.

suspect understands his or her rights and wants to make a statement or answer questions anyway. The waiver used by the Police Department in Kansas City, Missouri, reads:

> Before being asked any questions I have been told of my right to remain silent, that anything I say can and will be used against me in court, that I have the right to talk with a lawyer and to have the lawyer with me during questioning. I have also been told that if I cannot afford a lawyer that one will be appointed for me, at no cost to me, before I am questioned. I have also been told that I can stop talking at anytime. I understand all of these rights and I am willing to talk to you.[24]

Only after a suspect has signed the form, will a detective begin interrogation. Questions and answers have to be recorded in the detective's notebook. Geberth explains that this constant note taking is very necessary. He says,

> A favorite trick of defense counsel is … suggesting that there was some impropriety [improper behavior] on the part of the police in obtaining statements from a defendant. If the investigator has taken proper notes of the procedures utilized in obtaining any statements, along with notes of the responses of the suspect to these warnings, he or she will have eliminated a possible source of embarrassment in future court proceedings.[25]

Detectives always have the law and a possible trial in mind when they interrogate a suspect. Their ultimate goal is justice and that means a guilty verdict for the killer.

Many homicide detectives also videotape the procedure of reading Miranda warnings and waiving rights. According to

> **By the Numbers**
>
> **45%**
>
> **Percentage of murder cases solved in Baltimore, Maryland, in 2008**

Geberth, "a clock, which is visible in the background should be employed to record the total time of the interview."[26] The videotape is a permanent, legal record that the suspect was not coerced and voluntarily waived his or her rights. It is also a permanent record of the entire interrogation. It proves the

Confessions Wanted

Shane G. Sturman is an interrogation expert and certified forensic interviewer. He is the president of Wicklander-Zulawski and Associates, a forensic interview and training company for law enforcement personnel. He offers some tips about how to get admissions of guilt from a suspect:

Create the belief his guilt is known:
The suspect confesses because he believes that he is caught and wants to release his feelings of guilt.

Offering a face-saving option:
Minimize the seriousness of the crime…. Use rationalizations to allow the suspect to save face.

Using assumptive questions:
An assumptive question assumes that the suspect committed the crime and asks for an admission regarding some aspect of the crime. Examples of assumptive questions are as follows:

- What is the most number of cars you broke into in the last six months?
- Did you use the money for bills or was it for drugs?
- Did you plan this out or did you do it on the spur of the moment without thinking?
- Was this your idea or someone else's?

Shane G. Sturman, "Tools for Guiding the Confession," LawOfficer.com, August 22, 2008, www.lawofficer.com/news-and-articles/columns/sturman/tools_for_guiding_confession. html;jsessionid=31ACF8E8C4B15C3D417B34DC61FFE53A.

suspect's answers in case he or she denies making any of the statements later. It proves that the detective did not exhaust the suspect by questioning him or her for too many hours. Most detectives know that questioning cannot continue much longer than six or seven hours. Any longer would be legally considered a kind of force or coercion that makes statements untrustworthy in court.

The Truth in the Interrogation Room

Despite all these legal protections, however, detectives are often successful in getting suspects to respond to their questions during an interrogation. They may pretend to be sympathetic or resort to tricks and lies. Courts have ruled that lies and tricks are not coercion and not a violation of a suspect's rights. Good homicide detectives know how to use these tactics to get suspects to tell the truth.

William McCormack was a homicide detective in Toronto, Canada, during the 1970s. He had two suspects in a killing of a young man who had been gunned down in a store in an apparent robbery gone wrong. He knew that one suspect, Danny, had not pulled the trigger but had helped the suspected killer, Doug Parrack, after the murder. Because McCormack had little physical evidence; he needed to get Danny to talk. Danny, however, refused to cooperate.

During the interrogation, McCormack said calmly,

> I'm going to tell you something, and you'd better listen carefully: based on what I've learned tonight, by the time I've finished my investigation, I'm likely going to charge you—*just you*—with first-degree murder. So you've got a choice to make: either you continue to play the tough guy and take this beef all by yourself, or you smarten up and explain to my partner and me exactly what happened.[27]

Danny just swore at McCormack. The detective quietly began typing out a report. Then he started casually reading aloud what he had written, "Daniel … you have been arrested on a charge of first degree murder…. You are not obliged to say anything, unless you wish to do so, but whatever you say will be taken down in writing and may be given in evidence."[28]

Danny was horrified and broke down. "Wait a minute!" he cried, "You're not really going to—I didn't kill nobody!"[29] Then McCormack reassured him by pretending to be Danny's friend. He brought him some dinner and coffee. After he ate, Danny said he was ready to talk. At that point, McCormack told him his rights and warned him that he would be charged as an accessory to the murder. Then Danny confessed to his participation. He told McCormack that Parrack had borrowed his gun. He said Parrack had gone in the store and then run back to the car where Danny sat waiting for him. Parrack had yelled, "Let's get out of here! I blew his lights out!"[30]

Danny told the truth because he was afraid of facing a murder charge. McCormack knew all the time that Danny was not the killer, but his threat of a murder charge and then his kindness got at the truth. Danny preferred to go to prison as an accessory to murder rather than risk being sent to prison for life as a murderer. His statements helped to convict Doug Parrack of the killing.

Tricks of the Trade

Homicide detectives use many tricks to persuade suspects to talk to them. For instance, detectives try their best to prevent a suspect from asking for a lawyer in the interrogation room. If the suspect asks for a lawyer, then questioning has to stop immediately, so the detective may talk and talk, hoping the suspect will become involved and begin to respond to questions. If the suspect asks if he is under arrest, the detective may evade the question and ask if he wants to be under arrest. If the suspect

Once a lawyer is involved in an interrogation, it can be nearly impossible for detectives to get any information from a suspect.

says that maybe he or she should get a lawyer, then the detective might answer: "Maybe you should. But why would you need a lawyer if you don't have anything to do with this?"[31]

Another trick is to convince the suspect that the evidence against him is so good that lying is useless. Baltimore homicide detective Gene Constantine once gave a murder suspect the test used for drunk drivers. He told the suspect to close his eyes, stretch out his arms, and then touch his nose with a finger. Then he had him stand on one foot, and follow a moving finger with his eyes. Finally he announced that the suspect had failed a lie detector test. The suspect believed Constantine's trick that he had taken a lie detector test. He gave up and confessed to the murder.

Detectives may also claim to have evidence that they do not really have. A detective may say that the suspect's fingerprints were found on the murder weapon or that traces of the victim's blood are on the suspect's shoes or that witnesses have positively identified him. If two suspects are involved, a detective may walk one of them right past the interrogation room where the second is waiting. Then another detective will say that the first suspect talked and implicated the second. The first suspect is getting to go home, while the second will be charged with murder. Many suspects begin talking under circumstances like this. Detective

By the Numbers

26

Number of times more often fingerprints are used to solve a crime than DNA

Jay Landsman once used this trick, telling a suspect that his partner had named him as the killer. The suspect became furious and blurted, "He's the one that did it. He's the one."[32]

Once a suspect thinks he is doomed anyway, the detective gives him "the out" as a way to get him to confess. The out is an excuse, whatever story the suspect thinks will make the murder seem justified. The detective pretends to be sympathetic and interested in the suspect's welfare. Perhaps, says the detective, it was just self-defense or the victim deserved it. He or she offers the suspect a chance to tell his side of the story. A scared suspect, who knows he or she committed homicide, often breaks and tells a story of self-defense or gives an excuse, all the while admitting, of course, that he or she killed the victim. Landsman got a suspect to voice an excuse. He said, "I had the knife to her throat, but I didn't cut her. She must have moved or something."[33] It was a confession of murder, and the case was solved.

The End Justifies the Means

Some lawyers, politicians, and others believe that detective interrogation tactics are unfair and violate the rights of suspects. Geberth disagrees. He says, "Trickery and deceit are permissible and acceptable when dealing with a suspect in a murder case. Sometimes you only get one shot in these cases, and people don't give up information unless they have to…. I believe in trickery and deceit unless you are making an innocent person confess."[34]

CHAPTER 4

Cold Cases

With no witnesses and no suspects, Detective Curt Brannan had hit a dead end. His investigation of Brenda Salazar's murder in May 1997 had gone cold. A cold case is any investigation that has gone unsolved for about one year and is no longer being actively investigated. Unsolved homicide cases are never closed, but the investigation may stall. By the fall of 1997, for example, Brannan was not writing entries in his murder notebook anymore. He was not interviewing witnesses. He had nothing left to investigate. Although he would never file the case away, he knew that he might never solve the homicide. All he could do was hope for a break.

A Homicide with a Suspect

In August 1997, another young Hispanic female, fifteen-year-old Armida Garcia, was found raped and strangled with shoelaces in her home, also in Fort Worth, Texas. At the time, no one connected her murder with the Salazar case. A different homicide detective, Joe Thornton, was assigned to the investigation. Interviews with friends and family led Thornton to a neighborhood gang member named Andy James Ortiz. Ortiz had a long, violent criminal history. He had been accused of raping two teen girls in the past, but there had not been enough evidence for police to arrest him. Thornton's instinct told him that Ortiz was the killer. He thought to himself, "Now, how am I going to prove it?"[35]

The information about Andy Ortiz lead Thornton to a witness who had seen Ortiz on Garcia's front porch the night she was killed. Thornton also discovered friends of Garcia who said Ortiz had stalked her and pressured her for sex. Thornton also found a friend of Ortiz who claimed that Ortiz

The Search Warrant

For homicide detectives, search warrants are invaluable and necessary tools, not only to aid in the investigation, but also to ensure that the evidence can be used in court. Search warrants are legal authorizations for searches and seizures of evidence. The steps a detective must follow to obtain a search warrant are:

1. The detective writes a search warrant affidavit. It describes the facts that support probable cause to justify the search. The detective includes his or her name, the specific items to be searched for, the specific place and address of the search (a home, business, vehicle, person), and the probable cause, or reasons for the search. The affidavit must be very specific. At a business office, for example, the detective might indicate all the rooms, storage rooms, outside trash dumpsters, and even restrooms. Otherwise, these areas cannot be included in the search.

2. The detective appears before a judge and is formally sworn in as a witness to the facts listed in the affidavit.

3. The judge listens to the evidence of probable cause and reads the affidavit. At this time, the detective signs the affidavit in front of the judge. If the judge agrees that there is probable cause, then he or she signs and dates the affidavit, initials each page, and issues and signs the search warrant.

4. The search warrant is now an order of the court, and the detective is legally required and commanded to execute it promptly (usually within forty-eight to ninety-six hours). The detective serves the warrant to the person or persons whose property is to be searched. If the person refuses to admit the detective (including refusing to answer the door), the detective may enter the property by force.

5 Items listed in the search warrant are sought, seized, tagged as evidence, and carried away from the scene. An item cannot be seized if it is not listed in the search warrant, even if it is an illegal item. Usually, so that their search will not be too limited, detectives list small items (such as "sharp tools" or "ammunition") on the search warrant. That way, they can search in drawers, for example, and legally seize evidence such as bullets. It would be illegal to open a kitchen drawer during a search, for instance, if only a rifle was listed in the warrant. Because a rifle cannot fit into a drawer, the search of a drawer would be unreasonable. In addition, no property may be searched that is not specified in the warrant. For example, an unattached garage or shed or a vehicle in the driveway may not be searched if only the house is listed in the warrant.

6 The detective fills out the search warrant return, which is a formal record of everything that was seized during the search. One copy of the return is given to the person whose property was searched. Within twenty-four hours of the search, the original of the search warrant return is given to the judge who signed and issued the warrant. The detective signs the search warrant return in the presence of the judge. The judge also signs and dates it.

had told him that he had killed Garcia. It was enough for an arrest, but an interrogation of Ortiz failed to provide any further information. No DNA evidence from the crime scene linked Ortiz to the homicide. Then Ortiz's friend changed his story and denied being told about the murder. Thornton still believed Ortiz had killed Garcia. He took all his evidence to the prosecuting attorney and tried to persuade him that the evidence was strong enough to charge Ortiz with murder. The

Homicide detectives are often able to make a connection between murders because of similarities between the cases. In this instance, the knots tied in the wire that killed Minjarez were in the same bow shape as the knots in the shoelaces used to kill Armida Garcia.

prosecutor disagreed. Prosecutor Alan Levy of the Fort Worth District Attorney's Office explains, "We're looking at [a case] in terms of ... Is the case prosecutable? Not whether [a suspect] probably did something, but whether a jury is going to believe that they did it."[36] Thornton was frustrated and bitterly disappointed, but there was nothing he could do. Ortiz was released. Although Ortiz ended up going to jail that year for other gang-related crimes, he was not charged with Garcia's murder. At this point police had no reason to suspect that Garcia's murder was connected to Salazar's. That would take more time and another homicide.

Another Victim

In the summer of 2000, Detective Brannan was called to another murder of a young Hispanic girl. She was thirteen-year-old Krystal Minjarez, who had sneaked out of her house late one night to meet her boyfriend, Jaime. She had been raped and strangled with a piece of wire. Brannan's investigation uncovered Minjarez's address book and Jaime's phone number. It was the phone number of Andy James Ortiz. When Detectives Thornton and Brannanhappened to discuss this latest murder, both men suddenly realized that the Minjarez murder and the Garcia murder had a crucial clue in common, besides the name of Andy Ortiz. The knots tied in the wire that killed Minjarez were in the same bow shape of the knots in the shoelaces used to strangle Garcia. Thornton had always worried that Ortiz would commit more murders, especially since he was released from jail in 1999. Brannan said to Thornton, "We're going to get him now."[37]

> **By the Numbers**
>
> # 629
>
> **Number of cold cases solved by the New York City Cold Case Squad between 1996 and 2004**

Brannan got a search warrant and went to Ortiz's home. In his bedroom the detective and his team found pornographic videos of young Hispanic girls, and photos of sad-looking girls posed with Ortiz. They also found 126 scraps of paper, each bearing the name and phone number of a female. The detectives believed they had uncovered evidence of a serial killer. For weeks the homicide detectives worked to find the girls on the pieces of paper using the phone numbers. All were teens, and those whom detectives found had been stalked and threatened by Ortiz but not harmed. Unfortunately the detectives could not find many of the girls. Family addresses had changed; phones had been disconnected; people had moved away and left no forwarding information. Police efforts to check on these girls and their families led to dead ends. No one knew what happened to them.

Putting It All Together

As Brannan's investigation of Minjarez's murder continued, something suddenly clicked: What if Ortiz had been Brenda Salazar's killer, too? At twenty years old, she had not been a teen, but she was a young, pretty Hispanic woman. She had been strangled. Finally, Brannan remembered that the cord used to tie her hands had been in the same kind of knot as the

Fingerprint evidence can be checked quickly using a computer.

ligatures that killed Garcia and Minjarez. And he had DNA from Salazar's killer, taken during her autopsy. Playing his hunch, Brannan asked for DNA testing to check for a match between Ortiz and the sample taken from Salazar's body. He also asked for fingerprint comparisons between Ortiz and the fingerprint found on Salazar's abandoned car three years earlier.

Fingerprint evidence can be checked quickly using a computer database. In less than an hour, the fingerprint expert had an answer—the fingerprint from Salazar's car and Ortiz's left index finger were a match. It was not proof of homicide, but it was a strong piece of evidence. While he waited for DNA results, Brannan checked prison records to be sure Ortiz had not been incarcerated when Salazar was murdered. He had not. Then, five days later, the DNA test results were ready, and the lab reported a match to Ortiz. Brannan was thrilled. He said,

> Brenda's case had gone on for so long and had been such an intense investigation. And now, after all that, this is the guy. We've got him. There was no way he could explain both the fingerprint and the DNA.... No matter what happens on these other two cases... I'm going to be able to sit down with Brenda's family and tell them that the guy who did this is in jail.[38]

Brannan got an arrest warrant for Ortiz and invited Detective Thornton to come along for the arrest. Thornton was deeply satisfied for Garcia's sake, too. As he walked up to Ortiz after the arrest, he said only, "Remember me?"[39] The interrogation of Ortiz yielded very little information. Brannan was disappointed. He says, "I was convinced that he had done three murders. And I strongly believed then, as I do now, that there were other bodies out there. I was hoping and praying

Very Cold But Solved

In 2007 cold case homicide detectives solved their oldest, coldest case ever in Santa Ana, California. It was the 1964 murder of forty-seven-year-old Christine Elizabeth Wariner. She had been raped and beaten to death in a motel. Investigating detectives at the time found bloody fingerprints at the scene, but they never identified a suspect. As the decades passed, detectives searched different computerized fingerprint databases for a match, but they never found one. They had compared the fingerprints to more than two hundred different suspects, but all the suspects were cleared. Finally, in 2007, detectives submitted the prints to the FBI's national fingerprint database, which was established in 1999. There are 55 million fingerprint records in the FBI's Criminal Master File. This file yielded a match. It was to a sex offender named Charles Edward Faith Jr. He was about twenty-four years old at the time of the murder. At the time of his arrest, he was sixty-seven years old. He is now awaiting trial for Wariner's murder.

I could loosen him up and he would talk about those. I would have loved for him to tell me about the bodies out there that hadn't been found yet."[40] Ortiz, however, could not be persuaded to talk.

Justice

Detectives were never able to find out how many people Ortiz had killed, although they did get phone calls from girls after his arrest describing threats and rapes. Brannan took his evidence to Levy, and the prosecutor charged Ortiz with the murders of Brenda Salazar and Armida Garcia. In Garcia's case, a young girl came forward as an eyewitness. She told Brannan she had seen Ortiz running away from Garcia's house at the time of the murder but had been afraid to tell what she knew until

Ortiz was locked up. In separate trials, Ortiz was found guilty of the murders in October 2001. He was sentenced to two terms of life in prison. Ironically Ortiz was never convicted of killing Krystal Minjarez because the physical evidence was not strong enough, but her family knew that her death had led to solving the other murders. Minjarez's aunt said, "It's like she caught and convicted her own killer."[41] Ortiz still says, "I'm not going to admit to nothing that I didn't do."[42] Brannan, however, knows that his cold case is closed. Thornton can finally forget the case that he feared might remain unsolved forever. Homicide detectives hate cold cases because they mean that a killer goes free. But such unsolved investigations can linger for decades, despite the best efforts of homicide detectives.

> ## By the Numbers
>
> # 9,082
>
> **Number of unsolved New York City murders from 1985 to January 2007**

Cold Case Squads

Brannan solved his cold case himself, but in many large cities, special cold case squads take over cold cases and reinvestigate them. All the reports about witness interviews and leads are saved in the original case file. The physical evidence and the homicide detective's notebook are available and can be reviewed with fresh eyes and new ideas and plenty of time. Time is something that few regular homicide detectives have. They may be responsible for dozens of cases at any given time. Cold case squads do not have this problem. They are able to concentrate on a case for as long as it takes to solve it. Not all cold cases are solved, but some are.

In the report, "Cold Case Squads: Leaving No Stone Unturned," for the U.S. Bureau of Justice Assistance (BJA), a federal agency set up to help states and local governments strengthen their criminal justice systems, authors Ryan Turner and Rachel Kosa say that there are several reasons why cold cases could be solved today, even though they could not be

Cold case detectives have more time to revisit crime scenes and conduct door-to-door interviews.

closed at the time of the crime. First, witnesses and informants may come forward who were frightened or resistant in the past. Turner and Kosa explain that "with the passage of time ... witnesses may no longer feel intimidated by threats.... Individuals may have access to previously unavailable information, especially when a killer begins to boast about previous crimes. The relationship between suspects and witnesses may also have soured over time; in drug and gang-related homicides, the killer himself may have been killed."[43]

Other advantages for cold case detectives include improved DNA analysis and fingerprint technology. Turner and Kosa explain that these tools "were not available to law enforcement agencies in the past."[44] For example, the Federal Bureau of Investigation (FBI) established a national automated fingerprint database in 1999, which makes matching fingerprints now an easy task for law enforcement throughout the country. DNA analysis was first used to solve a crime in 1986 in England. Since 1997, more and more accurate analytic techniques have been developed for smaller and smaller DNA samples. Another tool is television and radio announcements that promote awareness of crimes and ask for tips. Turner and Kosa add, "The availability of telephone services (such as Crime Stoppers) that offer cash rewards for anonymous informants has increased the flow of cold case information to investigators."[45]

DNA Solves the Case

At times cold case investigations are easily solved because of new tools. In May 2007, in Buffalo, New York, cold case detectives Mary Gugliuzza and Charles Aronica were assigned a case from 1984. Their cold case involved an eighty-nine-year-old woman who had been raped and beaten to death in her home during a robbery. Blood evidence had been collected at the crime scene, but at that time, DNA technology and national databases were not available. Today the FBI maintains a national database where DNA profiles of known criminals are stored. Gugliuzza and Aronica found the blood evidence sample saved from 1984 in their storeroom. They submitted it

John List was caught after America's Most Wanted *featured his cold case on the show.*

for testing and got a match. The sample came from now-fifty-five-year-old Edward Richardson, a known criminal already in prison in Washington State. Gugliuzza and Aronica found proof that Richardson lived in the Buffalo area at the time of the murder. The detectives presented their evidence to a judge, received an arrest warrant, and extradited Richardson to Buffalo. In 2008 he was charged with the murder and scheduled for trial.

With the Help of the Public

In 1971 John List's wife, three children, and mother were found murdered in the List home in New Jersey. John List had disappeared, but he had left letters confessing to shooting his family. List was charged for the murders, but detectives could not find him. The case went cold, not because investigators did not know the identity of the killer, but because the killer had vanished.

In 1988 New Jersey detectives begged that year's new television show, *America's Most Wanted* to do a segment about John List. In 1989 the show aired the story. More than three hundred people called the tip line after the segment aired. One caller named a man called Robert Clark, living in Virginia. When detectives followed up on the tip, they found Robert Clark was really John List. He was positively identified by a scar behind his ear and then with fingerprints. List was tried, convicted, and sentenced to life in prison in 1990. He was tracked down and brought to justice because the New Jersey detectives never gave up and because the powerful tool of television was available to them.

Legwork and Brain Work Required

Cold cases usually take a lot of work, and detectives cannot expect to receive an important tip or a DNA match with every case. New York City's Cold Case and Apprehension Squad has about three dozen homicide detectives who concentrate on cold cases for as long as necessary. In August 2000, squad detective Wendell Stradford was assigned a cold case that occupied him

Cold case detectives spend a lot of time studying the original case notes on file.

71

for months: In December 1996, two drug dealers, Linda Leon and Esteban Martinez, were beaten, stabbed, and shot in the apartment they shared with their three little boys. The oldest boy, a six-year-old, called 911. The responding detectives suspected that the killings were drug related, but after an extensive investigation, they were unable to identify any suspects. Some fingerprints had been found in the apartment, but detectives had no suspects to match to the prints.

Stradford began his reinvestigation by reading over all the case notes, the lists of evidence, and the reports of witnesses interviewed. As he studied the information, he asked himself, "Who else we got to look at here? Who did we miss?"[46] He found one person—a man named Robert Mitchell, who had never been contacted or interviewed. Mitchell's cell phone number was in the phone records of calls to Martinez on the day of the murders. Since Mitchell's cell phone was listed at an address in Baltimore, Maryland, the first detectives had ignored him. They presumed that he was out of state at the time of the homicide and could not be a suspect. Stradford's discovery was not exactly a lead, but it was one small thing that had not been properly investigated.

Then Stradford read the statements taken from Leon and Martinez's children. The boys were so little at the time that they could give almost no information. But the oldest boy had pointed to an African American detective and said that the killer looked like him. The child said that he knew the killer. His name was Uncle Rob. If the child said Uncle Rob was the murderer and Robert Mitchell had called the parents on his cell phone, then Stradford was going to start his investigation by finding Mitchell. Stradford decided to go to Baltimore, Maryland. Two other detectives from the squad, Margie Yee and Steve Berger, drove down with him.

A Suspect But No Proof

In Baltimore, the police commissioner asked Detective Robert Snead to assist the New York investigation. On his computer, Snead searched for every Robert Mitchell who had ever been arrested in Baltimore. Finally he found a 1998 arrest record of a Robert Mitchell with the same address as the old cell phone, but it was an old address, not a current one. That Robert Mitchell was an African American who had been arrested in 1998 along with a friend named Tavon Blackmon. Perhaps Blackmon had information about the murders in New York. As it happened, Blackmon himself was currently wanted for murder in Baltimore, and Snead promised to call Stradford when they had found and arrested him.

Stradford and his team went back to New York. With the old address and the arrest record from 1998 that Snead had found, they now had enough information about Mitchell to do a computer search on him. They used a search tool called AutoTrack. AutoTrack is a database that contains records of any information ever officially entered about any person, whether by police, state agencies, or the federal government. The detectives entered the information they already had on Mitchell, such as his race, the one-time address that Snead had matched to the old cell phone number, the actual old cell phone number, and the criminal history from the Baltimore arrest record of 1998. With the AutoTrack search, the detectives found a new piece of information about Mitchell; it was an entry from the Department of Motor Vehicles (DMV). It gave an address for a woman named Keisha Washington with whom Mitchell was living when he registered his car. Stradford and his team had another name and another address.

Finally, in November, Baltimore police found and arrested Mitchell's friend Blackmon. During an interview with Detectives Snead and Berger, he admitted that Mitchell was his drug supplier. He said that Mitchell told him about driving to New York and killing a drug dealer and his wife. Mitchell told Blackmon that he; Keisha Washington; Keisha's twin brother, Kevin; and Kevin's girlfriend, Denise, had gone to the apartment to steal drugs and money. Mitchell had boasted that he bought a new car with his share of the money.

Miranda Rights and Cold Cases

Cold case homicide detectives face a particular problem trying to interrogate suspects from old homicide cases. If at any time in the past, the suspect refused to be interviewed and invoked his or her Miranda rights, detectives still cannot conduct an interview. New York cold case detective Vito Spano explains, "The days of beating someone up or threatening them ... are long gone. If you need this guy to make your case, and he says he wants an attorney, you're screwed. And the attachment is forever. If a Cold Case detective comes back five years later and tries to talk to him, it still applies. His attorney must be present."

Quoted in Stacy Horn, *The Restless Sleep: Inside New York City's Cold Case Squad*, New York: Penguin, 2005, p. 72.

Confessions

Stradford was now sure that Mitchell was the killer, but he needed evidence. The word of Blackmon, a drug-using, accused murderer was not credible enough for court. Snead came up with a trick. Keisha Washington had a son with Mitchell. Snead phoned Washington and pretended he was a social worker. In a series of phone calls, Snead made friends with Washington. He pretended he was trying to get Mitchell to pay her child support but needed to find him. Washington had broken up with Mitchell and had stopped using drugs. She wanted the money and trusted Snead. By March 2001, she agreed to meet with Snead to discuss where Mitchell might be. Stradford went along with Snead for the meeting, and the detectives told Washington who they really were and that they were investigating the homicides of Leon and Martinez. Washington was frightened, but the detectives assured her they were not going to arrest her. They just wanted her to come to the station for an interview.

In the interrogation room, Stradford worked to build a bond of sympathy with Washington. He talked to her about the three little boys who had been traumatized by the deaths of their parents. Washington felt guilty and broke down. She confessed that she and her brother's girlfriend, Denise, had helped tie up Leon and Martinez. Then the two women had taken the children into a bedroom to keep them quiet. Washington's brother, Kevin, and Mitchell had beaten and stabbed the parents to force them to tell where their money and drugs were hidden. Then Mitchell shot them. Washington also said, "Robert said, 'Come on let's go, we got enough. They dead. We got enough. They dead.' Then my brother Kevin said, 'No man, I want more than this, I'm risking my life. I want more than this.'… The children ran out the room, they started crying, they scream."[47] Kevin was currently in jail on another attempted murder charge. Washington did not know where Mitchell was.

More Evidence and Arrests

Stradford did not arrest Washington. He took her fingerprints and let her go home. Snead went back to Blackmon to identify Denise. She was Denise Ann Henderson, and her fingerprints were on file from a former job application. Later he got Kevin Washington's fingerprints from the jail. Stradford compared all three sets of fingerprints to the prints found at the crime scene. Keisha Washington's prints matched, but the other two did not. Stradford still needed more evidence.

In June 2001, Snead interrogated Kevin in jail and, knowing that Keisha had confessed, Kevin talked. He claimed Mitchell was the one truly at fault. Mitchell said they were only going to rob these people, not kill them. He admitted, however, that he had cut Leon with a knife. Then he said, "I'm sorry this had to happen and I wish Robert would be a man and admit killing those people. Because he started this and it's time for him to end it."[48]

The evidence was finally piling up. Stradford got an arrest warrant for Kevin Washington for the murders. Snead found

Fingerprints from the scene of the murder were compared to prints taken from Denise's job application.

the address where Henderson lived. He and Stradford arrested her, and she also confessed. Two of the four people who had been involved in the murders were in custody. Stradford and Snead arrested Keisha Washington at the end of June. By August, all three suspects had been brought to New York for trial. However, Stradford still had to apprehend Mitchell.

Eventually Sweet Success

On September 11, 2001, terrorists crashed planes into the World Trade Center in New York, the Pentagon in Virginia, and a field in Pennsylvania. The devastation in New York was the largest crime scene in the history of the United States, and every New York police officer was needed. Stradford had to put his work on Leon and Martinez's murder on hold as he was first assigned to guard the site of the attacks and then to the morgue where the victims' remains were brought. In Baltimore Snead continued to search for and identify the homes of Mitchell's family members.

At last, in October, Stradford joined Snead in a raid of Mitchell's mother's house. Mitchell was not there, and the mother was angry and uncooperative. Quickly the detectives came up with a good lie. They said, "Listen. Your family is in danger. Some of Mitchell's associates are after him, and you could get hurt."[49] The mother agreed to take the detectives to Mitchell's girlfriend's apartment. When they raided the apartment, they found Mitchell hiding under a bed.

During his interrogation, Mitchell blamed the killings on Kevin Washington. Mitchell was already wanted for crimes in Maryland and was sent to prison there. But Stradford got a New York arrest warrant prepared. As soon as Mitchell was ready for release in Maryland, he would be brought to New York to be tried for murder.

After many months of effort, Stradford had solved his cold case and apprehended all four of the killers. When the cases came to trial, he would testify for the prosecution and hope to see four convictions. Convictions make even the most difficult investigation worthwhile to a homicide detective.

CHAPTER 5

Into the Courtroom

In 2004 New York detective Wendell Stradford drove to Maryland one last time. He picked up suspect Robert Mitchell and drove him back to New York to be formally arrested and charged for the murders of Linda Leon and Esteban Martinez. Transporting a suspect to jail, whether across town or across the country, is the job of any detective who makes an arrest. It is the first step of the legal process that ends in a trial and, detectives hope, a conviction and a long prison sentence. Throughout the legal process, from bringing evidence to the district attorney's office to testifying at the trial, the detective is closely involved with the case.

Arrested, Booked, and Arraigned

In New York City, as in many other U.S. cities, detectives first take their suspects to a holding cell in their precinct and notify the district attorney (DA) or assistant district attorney (ADA). At this point of an arrest for murder, say detectives, "the clock starts ticking."[50] No one in the United States can be held without formal charges. To hold a suspect, law enforcement and the courts must formally charge him or her within twenty-four to forty-eight hours of the arrest. First the detective has to fill out official forms and reports about the arrest and then take the suspect to Central Booking. Often, the DA or ADA accompanies the detective, so as to be ready to stand before a judge to state the charges. The suspect is booked into the booking facility, fingerprinted, searched, and photographed. Within hours, it is time for his or her arraignment.

Arraignment court is the place where a judge informs the suspect of the charges, explains his or her legal rights, appoints

a lawyer for the suspect if necessary, and allows the suspect to plead guilty or not guilty. It is also the place where bail is set so that a criminal suspect can go home until trial, if they can pay the bail. Homicide suspects, however, are almost never allowed bail. District attorneys will not agree to bail for murder suspects, and most judges will not grant it because the charge is too serious and the flight risk for the suspect is deemed to be high. After arraignment, most murder suspects are held in jail until the time of their trial.

During an arraignment a suspect is informed of his or her rights and the charges against him or her.

Bargaining for Testimony

While they wait for the trial, the DA and the homicide detective work closely together to gather and sort the evidence that will be used in court, as well as to set up a witness list of people who will testify. This is also the time that a plea bargain may be made with the defendant. Detectives have no authority to agree to plea bargains; that is the function of the district attorney's office. However, detectives will inform DAs about people who may have valuable information to trade for a reduced prison sentence.

Stradford, for example, helped to arrange a deal in the trial of Kevin Washington. Stradford and ADA Nancy Borko arranged a plea agreement with Keisha Washington and Denise Henderson. The ADA agreed to charge them with robbery (instead of murder) and offered six to twelve years in prison. The women could have received life sentences if they were charged with and found guilty of murder. In exchange, the women agreed to testify against Kevin in his murder trial and to plead guilty to the robbery charges. At Kevin Washington's trial, which took place in 2003, Stradford testified for the prosecution, and both Keisha Washington and Henderson told the truth about Kevin's involvement. He was found guilty.

After the judge sentenced him to seventy-five years in prison, Washington glared angrily at Stradford. Stradford blew him a kiss in return. He was glad about the outcome. The family of Linda Leon thanked Stradford for solving the case and getting justice for her and the children. One cousin said, "We thought it was a lost cause."[51] It was a conclusion that left Stradford with a deep sense of satisfaction.

Avoiding Discovery Pitfalls

A trial is never guaranteed to lead to a conviction. Homicide detectives are well aware that anything can happen at trial, and that defense attorneys will do their best to call the best evidence into doubt. During the process called discovery, the prosecution must give copies of all the formal evidence that will be used in court to the defense. This includes detectives' investigation files. These files include formal records of physical evidence that was collected. They include notes and notebooks about the case. They include the forms that detectives complete

During the discovery process prosecutors must turn over all of the detective's files to the defense.

describing each interview. Basically, everything a detective does during the investigation is recorded on an official form. In New York City's Cold Case Squad, the forms are called DD5s (for Detective Division 5). Today DD5s are written and stored on computers. In some states, the detective's personal notes must also be turned over to the defense. In other states, like New York, personal notes are not included in discovery, and only forms, such as DD5s, must be turned over to the defense. New York detective Vito Spano says that "anything you wrote on those 5s may be used by the defense as ammunition to attack your case."[52] For this reason, detectives are careful about what they include in a DD5.

Spano explains, "Criminal investigations go in many different directions in the beginning. As the investigation progresses, issues become clearer."[53] If, for example, detectives wrote up a DD5 suggesting that they suspected a husband in a murder and later realized that the evidence implicated a boyfriend, that early DD5 could be used by the boyfriend's defense attorney during trial. The attorney could try to establish doubt for the jury by pointing out that the detectives had suspected the husband at first. Spano says, "Now the prosecution has to explain away the [seeming] inconsistencies in the case."[54] Therefore, most detectives do not write up DD5s for suspects until they feel sure that they have accurately determined what happened. They try to prove or disprove witness statements before they write up formal reports. Nevertheless, before a case goes to the district attorney, the formal reports must be completed. A case file for a homicide may end up with dozens of these formal reports of evidence collection, witness interviews, and suspect statements.

Before a case goes to trial, a homicide detective organizes the reports in the case file and makes sure that his or her notes are complete. Any piece of evidence that a detective fails to give to the prosecutor is evidence not given to the defense. If evidence is overlooked or left out, the defense attorney may accuse the detective or the district attorney of hiding evidence. The defense may claim that evidence that would cast doubt on the suspect's guilt was deliberately withheld. Even if the suspect is guilty, the legal system may free a defendant under such circumstances, citing that the trial was not a fair one under the law. So detectives, who want to see convictions, try hard not to miss anything when they give their evidence to the district

Prizing Honesty and Skill

Stephen B. Tabeling is a retired Baltimore homicide detective and supervisor. He came out of retirement to train detectives and police officers in "the art of testifying in court." Tabeling explains, "Court testimony skills must be of [the] highest level of proficiency. I tell these guys, when you get on the witness stand, you not only tell the truth. You have to paint a word picture for the judge and the jury so they will think as if they were there."

Quoted in John B. O'Donnell, Jim Haner, and Kimberly A. C. Wilson, "To Veteran Officer, a 'Sad State of Affairs,'" *Baltimore Sun*, October 1, 2002, www.baltimoresun.com/news/maryland/bal-te.tabeling01oct01,0,5716787.story.

attorney. Once the files are turned over, the homicide case is under the control of the prosecuting district attorney. The detective is no longer in charge. He or she must now prepare to be a witness and testify in court for the prosecution.

Waiting to Testify

Testifying is a very important part of a homicide detective's job. Detectives want to do their best in court. Crime writer Stacy Horn explains,

> Detectives want to testify. They're the ones who figured out who did it, who hunted the murderer down and pulled him out of the life he didn't deserve to be enjoying. Standing up in court … in a sometimes year-long process to explain exactly what they did in front of colleagues and friends, and the victim's family and friends, is their one moment to fulfill a very human need to let it be known that they, too, were a part of a job well done.[55]

A homicide detective is not allowed to attend the whole trial because he or she is a witness. Witnesses are legally barred from listening to court proceedings so that their testimony cannot be influenced by other witness testimony. Because of this, homicide detectives spend most of their time during the trial waiting outside the courtroom. Journalist David Simon says,

> From crime scene to conviction, the courthouse is the only part of the process in which the detective becomes a passive participant, a player wholly dependent on the decisions of others. A detective is there to testify and otherwise serve the lawyers in any way he can…. [The detective is] responsible for showing up on time with the right evidence and the right witnesses…. Court time for a detective is a strange limbo, a period of non-existence that is only briefly interrupted when he is called to testify.[56]

Detectives often carry bags of physical evidence from the evidence room to the courthouse. If an important witness fails to show up, the detective will go to his or her home and escort the witness to court. The rest of the time, detectives sit, do crossword puzzles, read newspapers, and wait for trial breaks so that they can ask the district attorney how things are going. They cannot even work on other ongoing murder investigations because their presence is required at the trial.

Testifying with Accuracy

Prosecutors need homicide detectives in every murder trial to lay the groundwork for the case. The detective usually testifies about the crime scene and what was found there, the witnesses and how they were discovered, and any statements made by the defendant. Many prosecutors say that a detective's testimony can make or break a case. Jurors often rely on the detective's testimony for a factual and objective description of the crime and need to feel comfortable that the testimony is unbiased, accurate, and trustworthy. The detective has to be well prepared and able to answer calmly any question from the prosecutor or the defense lawyer.

Detailed notes taken at a crime scene can help a detective who is testifying seem reliable and thorough.

Before the trial, detectives carefully read over their notes and files to refamiliarize themselves with the case. This is necessary because trials usually happen months or even years after the arrest. During that time, detectives have handled many other homicide investigations and may have forgotten the details of the particular case on trial.

Many detectives bring their notes or copies of their notes with them when they take the stand to testify. Although the notes allow them to look up a detail that they may not remember, the notes can sometimes present a problem. The defense lawyer is allowed to see the notes since they have been brought into the courtroom. If the notes contain comments about other possible suspects, the defense lawyer can use them to establish doubt about the guilt of the defendant. Therefore, some detectives make copies of their notes that leave out any information that is not needed for testimony. Baltimore homicide detective Donald Worden has a different approach; he memorizes the details of his cases. When a disbelieving defense attorney once asked him how he could testify without notes, Worden replied coolly, "I just remember things. Ask your question."[57]

Being the Perfect Witness

Remaining cool, polite, and professional on the witness stand is critical for a homicide detective. Phil Evans, a prosecutor in Norfolk, Virginia, says that prosecutors cannot win cases unless detectives do a good job on the witness stand. In the article "Homicide Investigators and Prosecutors: An Essential Alliance," for the newsletter, *Inside the Tape*, Evans offers the following tips for detectives:

> You are a salesman. You must sound convincing and believe in what you are testifying to. Do not respond in a tone that sounds like you are apologizing for the defendant even being charged with the crime.
>
> Your case report is not a foreign object. If you bring it to court be prepared to locate the documents in it when called.

It does not improve your credibility [believability] with the court or a jury if you cannot locate a rights advisal [Miranda] form in your own file.

Who is your audience? The judge in a bench trial and a jury of 12 in a jury trial. Receive the questions from the Commonwealth Attorney but turn and give your answer to the judge/jury. Remember that the prosecutor does not vote for guilt or innocence.

Maintain control and think before you speak. A good defense attorney has a reason for not only what questions he asks, but how he asks them. For example, if your are testifying on direct examination with respect to the defendant's confession then the defense attorney is either going to attack the voluntariness of the statement, the accuracy of the statement, or the existence of prior "undocumented" statements [for example, statements of innocence early in the interrogation].

You should be the professional. Listen to the tone of the defense attorney: reassure the jury of the correctness of your testimony.

When the defense gives you an opening, jump through it. Restate the basis of your direct testimony. For example:

Q. Isn't it true that the defendant asked to talk with his attorney?
(Routine Answer): No.
(Better Answer): Sir, the defendant was advised of his rights and never asked to speak to an attorney. He said he wanted to tell us what happened.

WE DO NOT WANT TO START VOLUNTEERING INFORMATION THAT WAS NOT PART OF YOUR DIRECT EXAMINATION.

THIS IS AN OPPORTUNITY TO REEM-
PHASIZE YOUR DIRECT EXAMINATION,
NOT VENTURE INTO PARTS OR AREAS
UNKNOWN.

Do not allow yourself to become visibly annoyed at the
defense counsel. Remember that there are many people
on juries who do not trust the police and are willing to
believe a tall tale if they have something to base it on
(such as seeing you lose your temper or control).[58]

Tiny Details Matter

At times, it can be difficult for a homicide detective to remain
calm on the witness stand, especially during cross-examination
by the defense lawyer. The lawyer may question any piece of
the detective's evidence or try to prove that the detective made
mistakes in the investigation. Vincent E. Henry, an associate
professor of criminal justice at Pace University in New York
and a retired New York City police sergeant, wrote *Death Work:
Police, Trauma, and the Psychology of Survival*. In it he quotes a
homicide detective who learned the hard way how important

*Defense attorneys
may use different
methods, like
making him or her
read and talk about
prior testimony, to
rattle a detective on
the stand.*

every bit of documentation in a detective's notes can be at trial:

I had a case … a homicide in Manhattan from 2 years ago. Every time you testify, you learn…. In my notes from the scene I had the perp's [perpetrator's] name and address. I was asked [in court], "Where did you get that information?" Well, it was given to me by someone at the scene. I don't recall who. Now, at the trial, all the cops at the scene—the patrol supervisor, the detectives, everybody—said they didn't have that information but it turned up in my notes somewhere along the line. Somebody had it because somebody gave it to me, but I don't know who. So now, when I take down anyone's name or ask anyone what happened, I write, "advised by so-and-so."[59]

It was a very small detail, but defense lawyers can use small details to undermine a detective's believability. Any time that a detective has to say "I don't remember" or "I didn't check that out," he or she looks less professional to the jury.

Attacked by the Defense

In another case, Baltimore homicide detective Richard Garvey was testifying about the murder of a woman named Lena Lucas. She was a cocaine user who had been found stabbed and shot to death in her apartment. Her boyfriend, Robert Frazier, was on trial for her murder. Frazier was a cocaine dealer who sometimes had Lucas keep drugs and weapons for him. Detectives knew that Frazier had also killed another person that same night, the father of his drug-dealing associate, Vincent Booker. However, the judge had ruled that the second homicide could not be mentioned because it would prejudice the jury and perhaps lead to an unfair trial. The defense lawyer, Paul Polansky, wanted to create doubt about Frazier's guilt by suggesting that someone else, possibly Booker, had killed Lucas.

During his testimony, Detective Garvey described the crime scene for the prosecutor. He explained that there had been no signs of forced entry into the apartment; he described the scratches on the headboard of the bed where Lucas was found; he pointed out the details in every crime-scene photograph for the jury; and he described the street lighting outside the apartment building because a witness had identified Frazier on the street that night.

In cross-examination, Polansky questioned the thoroughness of Garvey's investigation. He pointed to one of the crime-scene

Aiding the Defense, According to the Law

During discovery, defense lawyers often want to interview the prosecution's witnesses. Discovery rules, however, vary from state to state. In California, for example, the defense is not allowed to demand the prosecution's witness list, but detectives must cooperate with the lawyer's efforts to speak to witnesses. Sheriff Leroy Baca of Los Angeles County explains,

> While preparing for trial, the defense will often seek to interview the prosecution's witnesses. In years past, the defense would have full access to the names, addresses and telephone numbers of the witnesses, but ... that is no longer the case. However, Homicide investigators are obliged to notify the witnesses that the defense wishes to speak with them. Investigators will neither encourage nor discourage the witnesses from meeting with the defense. It is up to each witness to make that decision for themselves.

Sheriff Leroy Baca, "Anatomy of a Murder Investigation," *LACounty Murders*, January 20, 2005, http://lacountymurders.com/articles/article-anatomy.html.

photos of the floor near the bed of the victim. It showed a pack of cigarettes and an ashtray. He asked Garvey, "Did you ever determine Ms. Lucas was a smoker?"

Garvey was stuck. He knew the cigarettes were not important, but he had no notes about them. He had to say, "I can't recall if I did or not."

Polansky jumped on this admission. He said, "Do you think that might have been of some significance?"

Garvey handled the situation as best he could. He replied, "I'm sure the question came up during the investigation. Obviously, the answer didn't have any significance."[60] Still, Polansky implied that the real murderer remained unidentified because Garvey's investigation was sloppy and ignored key evidence.

Garvey remained outwardly calm, but he was upset that he could not prove that his investigation had been thorough, that he had not ignored the possibility of any other suspects. Fortunately the exchange did not damage the case against Frazier. During a break, Garvey apologized to the prosecutor for not having an easy explanation about the cigarettes. He was fairly sure that he had been told that the cigarettes belonged to Lucas, but he could not remember how he knew they were unimportant. Then he went to find Lucas's daughter and asked her if they had belonged to her mother. They had. The prosecutor called the daughter to the stand later to testify that the victim had smoked that kind of cigarettes. Frazier was convicted of Lucas's murder.

The More Details, the Better

It is during the trial that a homicide detective's notes and crime-scene notebook are critically important. Canadian detective William McCormack says, "In Homicide, reliance on observations recorded in notebooks is especially strong. You learn to ignore nothing and to jot down everything.... The last thing you want is for a defence lawyer to ask you a question the answer to which you ought to know but can't recall."[61] Once during a murder trial, McCormack's partner,

George Thompson, was being grilled by the defense lawyer about the crime scene. The lawyer was trying to force a response that would prove a sloppy investigation. Thompson, however, testified perfectly. McCormack says that his partner always had "an accurate and detailed answer." Then, McCormack relates, "With mounting frustration, the lawyer tried to break George's stride by asking him a question he was sure would stump him: 'And I suppose, Sergeant Thompson, that if I were to ask you the wattage of the bulb that had been inserted into the kitchen light fixture, you'd know the answer to that question, too. Is that correct?'" Calmly, Thompson found the correct page in his notebook. He answered, "Yes, sir. It was a one-hundred watt bulb. Sylvania … frosted."[62] The lawyer gave up and had no further questions.

In the Name of Justice

If the ultimate goal of the homicide detective is justice for the murder victim, then helping the prosecution to get a conviction is the final step in the detective's job. However, detectives know that many homicide cases will go unsolved. They know that arrests do not necessarily mean convictions in a court of law. They know that convictions do not always mean long prison sentences. Much of their investigative work is tedious

Television shows, such as CSI, give the impression that all killers can be caught and convicted or that DNA and fingerprint evidence are always available. However, these expectations are not based on reality.

and even boring and still may lead to a dead end. The public often criticizes their work and points out their failures. Citizens lie to them, and witnesses to crimes refuse to come forward or to testify. Because of television, juries expect to see DNA and fingerprint evidence at every trial. Also because of television, everyone thinks every killer can be identified, caught, and convicted. Sometimes, the job of the homicide detective can feel thankless, but detectives still take pride in bringing murderers to justice.

Once, Baltimore homicide detective Dave Brown was in the courtroom when the jury brought in a guilty verdict against two young men who had killed an elderly minister during a robbery. Brown was the detective who had investigated the case and arrested the men. One of the defendants turned toward Brown, yelled an ugly curse word at him, and shouted "You happy now?" For a moment, the courtroom was silent. Brown calmly replied in the hush, "Yes, I'm pleased."[63]

Notes

Introduction: Murder Specialists

1. Vernon J. Geberth, *Practical Homicide Investigation: Tactics, Procedures, and Forensic Techniques*, 3rd ed., Boca Raton, FL: CRC Press, 1996, p. vi.

Chapter 1: Called to the Scene

2. Geberth, *Practical Homicide Investigation*, p. xxxii.

3. Geberth, *Practical Homicide Investigation*, p. xxxiv.

4. Thomas McKenna and William Harrington, *Manhattan North Homicide*, New York: St. Martin's, 1996, p. 28.

5. McKenna and Harrington, *Manhattan North Homicide*, pp. 28–29.

6. David Simon, *Homicide: A Year on the Killing Streets*, Boston, MA: Houghton Mifflin, 1991, pp. 69–70.

7. Geberth, *Practical Homicide Investigation*, p. 105.

Chapter 2: Making a Case

8. Simon, *Homicide*, p. 385.

9. Quoted in Simon, *Homicide*, p. 502.

10. Quoted in Simon, *Homicide*, p. 512.

11. Quoted in Tim Madigan, Deanna Boyd, and Melody McDonald, "To Catch a Killer," Star-Telegram.com, www.star-telegram/killer, chapter 2.

12. Quoted in Miles Corwin, *Homicide Special: A Year with the LAPD's Elite Detective Unit*, New York: Holt, 2003, p. 95.

13. Quoted in Corwin, *Homicide Special*, pp. 96.

14. Quoted in Corwin, *Homicide Special*, pp. 96–97.

15. McKenna and Harrington, *Manhattan North Homicide*, p. 78.

Chapter 3: Interrogations and Arrests

16. Quoted in Simon, *Homicide*, p. 32.

17. Quoted in Simon, *Homicide*, p. 146.

18. Quoted in Simon, *Homicide*, pp. 144, 146.

19. Quoted in Simon, *Homicide*, p. 146.

20. Geberth, *Practical Homicide Investigation*, p. 84.

21. McKenna and Harrington, *Manhattan North Homicide*, p. 158.

22. McKenna and Harrington, *Manhattan North Homicide*, pp. 42–44.

23. Quoted in Geberth, *Practical Homicide Investigation*, p. 57.

24. Kansas City, Missouri, Police Department, "Procedural Instruction: Miranda Warning and Miranda Waiver," Kansas City, Missouri, Police Department, February 4, 2002, www.kcpd.org/masterindex/Files/pi/PI0204.pdf.

25. Geberth, *Practical Homicide Investigation*, p. 95.

26. Geberth, *Practical Homicide Investigation*, p. 141.

27. William McCormack and Bob Cooper, *Life on Homicide: A Police Detective's Memoir*, Toronto, Canada: While Knight Publications, 2004, pp. 84–85.

28. McCormack and Cooper, *Life on Homicide*, p. 85.

29. Quoted in McCormack and Cooper, *Life on Homicide*, p. 85.

30. Quoted in McCormack and Cooper, *Life on Homicide*, p. 87.

31. Simon, *Homicide*, p. 203.

32. Quoted in Simon, *Homicide*, p. 555.

33. Quoted in Simon, *Homicide*, p. 556.

34. Quoted in Thomas J. Lueck, "Ruling in L.I. Case Casts a Glare on Tricks Used in Interrogations," *New York Times*, December 23, 2007, http://query.nytimes.com/gst/fullpage.html?res=950CE1D91039F930A15751C1A9619C8B63&sec=&spon=&pagewanted=all.

Chapter 4: Cold Cases

35. Quoted in Madigan, Boyd, and McDonald, "To Catch a Killer," chapter 7.

36. Quoted in Madigan, Boyd, and McDonald, "To Catch a Killer," chapter 8.

37. Quoted in Madigan, Boyd, and McDonald, "To Catch a Killer," chapter 14.

38. Quoted in Madigan, Boyd, and McDonald, "To Catch a Killer," chapter 19.

39. Quoted in Madigan, Boyd, and McDonald, "To Catch a Killer," chapter 20 .

40. Quoted in Madigan, Boyd, and McDonald, "To Catch a Killer," chapter 20.

41. Quoted in Madigan, Boyd, and McDonald, "To Catch a Killer," chapter 23.

42. Quoted in Madigan, Boyd, and McDonald, "To Catch a Killer," chapter 23.

43. Ryan Turner and Rachel Kosa, "Cold Case Squads: Leaving No Stone Unturned," *BJA Bulletin*, July 2003, p. 3.

44. Turner and Kosa, "Cold Case Squads," p. 5.

45. Turner and Kosa, "Cold Case Squads," p. 5.

46. Quoted in Stacy Horn, *The Restless Sleep: Inside New York City's Cold Case Squad*, New York: Penguin, 2005, p. 78.

47. Quoted in Horn, *The Restless Sleep*, p. 88.

48. Quoted in Horn, *The Restless Sleep*, p. 91.

49. Quoted in Horn, *The Restless Sleep*, p. 100.

Chapter 5: Into the Courtroom

50. Quoted in Horn, *The Restless Sleep*, p. 222.

51. Quoted in Horn, *The Restless Sleep*, p. 230.

52 Quoted in Horn, *The Restless Sleep*, p. 191.

53. Quoted in Horn, *The Restless Sleep*, p. 191.

54. Quoted in Horn, *The Restless Sleep*, p. 191.

55. Horn, *The Restless Sleep*, p. 139.

56. Simon, *Homicide*, p. 460.

57. Quoted in Simon, *Homicide*, p. 245.

58. Phil Evans, "Homicide Investigators and Prosecutors: An Essential Alliance," *Inside the Tape* (newsletter), January 2008, www.insidethetape.com/news letter-1.htm

59. Quoted in Vincent E. Henry, *Death Work: Police, Trauma, and the Psychology of Survival*, New York: Oxford University Press, 2004, pp. 186–87.

60. Quoted in Simon, *Homicide*, p. 474.

61. McCormack and Cooper, *Life on Homicide*, p. 96.

62. McCormack and Cooper, *Life on Homicide*, pp. 96–97.

63. Quoted in Simon, *Homicide*, p. 464.

For More Information

Books

Barry M. Baker, *Becoming a Police Officer: An Insider's Guide to a Career in Law Enforcement*. Lincoln, NE: iUniverse, 2006. Retired Baltimore, Maryland, police detective Barry Baker's book is written for young people who are interested in a career in law enforcement. Baker describes both the satisfaction and the difficulties of the job, as well as the skills and character needed to be successful.

Milton Meltzer, *Case Closed: The Real Scoop on Detective Work*. New York: Orchard, 2001. This book follows police detectives, crime lab investigators, and private detectives as they work on cases of embezzlement, murders, organized crime, and more.

Carey Scott, *Crime Scene Detective*. New York: DK, 2007. In this easy-to-read book, readers can follow the work of a whole team of detectives and criminal scientists as they investigate different kinds of crime scenes. Do-it-yourself activities help readers to identify the important clues at crime scenes.

Richard Worth, *Homicide*. New York: Chelsea House, 2008. This book explores the history of homicide and the efforts of law enforcement to solve murder cases, from early times to modern day. It includes discussions of criminal motives, evidence collection, and court prosecutions of killers.

Internet Sources

Julia Layton, "How Crime Scene Investigation Works," HowStuffWorks, http://science.howstuffworks.com/csi.htm. Visitors can read about how lie detectors work, how polygraph examiners are trained, and even visit a special Kid's Zone that discusses lie detector tests.

———, "How Police Interrogation Works," HowStuffWorks, http://people.howstuffworks.com/police-interrogation.htm. In this detailed article about police interrogations, visitors are introduced to interview techniques and psychological tactics. The article includes a real interrogation in which a detective uses his skills to get a confession.

WhatDoYouWant2Be? "Michael Bathem: Homicide Detective," WhatDoYouWant2Be? www.whatdoyouwant2be.org/profiles/MichaelBathem_A.html. Read a short interview with a Los Angeles homicide detective. He describes daily life on the job and what he enjoys about his work.

Web Sites

American Polygraph Association (www.polygraph.org). This Web site describes how lie detectors work and how polygraph examiners are trained. There is a "Kidz Zone" for grades one through five and a "Learning Zone" for grades six through twelve.

Los Angeles Police Department (www.lapdonline.org). This is the official Web site of the Los Angeles Police Department. It offers information about the men and women on the police force, the most wanted criminals in the area, videos about evidence storage and the dog squad, crime maps of Los Angeles, and much more.

Index

Picture Credits

Cover photo: Image copyright Olivier La Queinec, 2009. Used under license from Shutterstock.com

About the Author

Toney Allman holds degrees from Ohio State University and the University of Hawaii. She currently lives in Virginia where she enjoys a rural lifestyle and researching and writing books for students.

DATE DUE	BORROWER'S NAME